THE PATHWAY HOME

A JOURNEY INTO LIGHT

Carole Sanborn Langlois

COPYRIGHT © 1996 BY CAROLE SANBORN LANGLOIS
All rights reserved

No portion of this book may be reproduced in any form without written permission from the publisher, except for brief quotations embodied in literary articles or reviews.

Original Painting by:
Ann Marie Eastburn
Copyright © 1996

Typesetting :   Yvan Grenier
                 Montréal (Québec) Canada

Published by:

THAT'S THE SPIRIT PUBLISHING COMPANY

U. S. :   P.O. Box 2503
                   Ft Lauderdale, Fl   33303-2503
                   Tel/fax : (954) 522-8317
                   Internet :   whtlite@icanect.net (Carole)

CANADA :   3500 Fallowfield Rd, P.O. Box 290145
                   Nepean, Ontario, Canada   K2J 4A9
                   Tel/fax : (613) 825-0259

Printed in Canada

ISBN 0-9637744-3-3

DEDICATION

In April 1994, I was awakened one night from a deep sleep.

As I sat up in bed wondering what had awakened me so suddenly,

I felt a presence in my room.

As I looked towards the foot of my bed, I saw a line of writing

in the air. In the middle, there seemed to be

a picture of a lady in a long gown.

I could not read it, so I verbally asked, "What does it say?"

And a voice answered :

**DEDICATED TO MOTHER MARY
AND HER VISION OF
THE WORLD IN TRANSITION**

I knew I had just been given the dedication for my next book!

TABLE OF CONTENTS

FOREWORD	11
ACKNOWLEDGMENTS	15
NOTE TO READERS	17
MESSAGE FROM MOTHER MARY & ST. JOSEPH	19
INTRODUCTION	21

Chapter One
ENDINGS AND NEW BEGINNINGS 29

Chapter Two
RELEASING THE DENSITY 39

Chapter Three
PATHWAY TO ASCENSION, SANANDA 49

Chapter four
TRANSFORMATIONS, ST.-GERMAIN 61

Chapter five
THE HIGHER SELF, ARCHANGEL MICHAEL 71

Chapter six
AWAKENING SPIRITUALLY, SANANDA 81

Chapter seven
LOVE AND COMPASSION, MOTHER MARY 93

Chapter eight
AN AWAKENING HUMANITY, ST.-GERMAIN 111

Chapter nine
**MOTHER EARTH AND HER INHABITANTS,
ARCHANGEL GABRIEL** 121

Chapter ten
POWER OF LOVE, SANANDA 135

Chapter eleven
RELEASING PAST THOUGHT PATTERNS 147

Chapter twelve
THE COMPLETION OF OUR MISSION 155

REQUEST FROM MOTHER MARY 167

ABOUT THE AUTHOR 169

Carole Sanborn Langlois

THE PATHWAY HOME

A JOURNEY INTO LIGHT

FOREWORD

As we move closer to the end of the century and the Time of Revelations mentioned in the Bible of nearly every religion on Earth, I consider my first book, **SOUL RESCUE - Help on the Way Home to Spirit,** published in 1994, a very timely book. It holds an important message for humanity...to help release the fear of dying. It contains a loving message of faith and hope, and finally the understanding and inner acceptance that there is no death...only a continuation of life in a much better world, a world from which we originally came.

Spirit gave me the title for the second book, and said it would contain the information needed to help those who had been awakened by the reading of SOUL RESCUE and other newly awakening souls, to continue their Spiritual growth. It would also aid in triggering the remembrance of their soul identity, and the understanding and acceptance that they are a soul first and foremost : **A Spiritual being having a human experience in a physical body.**

Those of us who have been awakened to the knowledge of whom we are as the soul are truly blessed, and now it is our turn to help others in the awakening process.

We are living in the most important time in the history of humanity, as our beloved Mother Earth is being taken back into the fifth dimension, and we are ascending with her.

We have arrived at a point in the history of the evolution of Mother Earth when we, as inhabitants of the planet, have a decision to make. We must make the choice of whether to allow our soul, the real owner of our physical body, to complete the mission it came to fulfill or, as the ego, insist on retaining control and refusing all Spiritual awakening.

There will be many souls leaving the physical body because they refuse to stay in a vehicle that is no longer of any use to them! The message received from the Ascended Masters in May, 1994, was: "As of the beginning of July, expect a mass exodus of souls who will be leaving the physical body to return to the World of Spirit, as they are not being permitted by the ego to finish the tasks they chose to complete in this incarnation!"

Many of these souls are in young bodies and will pass to spirit through tragic circumstances. Some of them will be well known. They have unconsciously chosen to leave their physical bodies in a way that will make the greatest impact on the consciousness of all humanity, in the hope that we may finally realize that something important, over which we have no control, is happening on the planet.

When we received this message, it confirmed something I had been sensing for several months. I had felt that Jacqueline Kennedy Onassis would be one of the first of a long line of high profile people who, on a soul level, had chosen to leave the planet at this time in order to give a lesson to humanity. She prepared her return to The Spirit Realms in the most loving, graceful, and dignified way possible. For more than thirty years, everyone knew and admired this courageous lady. She stood tall during all of the devastating experiences in her earthly life. We were all deeply touched as once again, her *undaunted spirit rose to the occasion, and lovingly prepared herself and everyone around her, for her imminent physical departure from the Earth plane.*

Most of this book is channeled by my Beloved Ascended Masters. I also wanted to share some of my own experiences and insights into my ongoing Spiritual work with you, many of whom I have been blessed to have met personally.

I pray that through the reading of this book, you take a quantum leap forward into the Light. May your **LIGHT BODY** *glow so brightly that you become the* **Beacon of Light you were originally meant to be!** *Our brothers and sisters on the planet will feel this Light, leave their chrysalis, and become the beautiful butterflies they truly are.*

ACKNOWLEDGMENTS

To all my friends on Planet Earth – they know who they are – who have encouraged me over the past year to "**hurry up and finish that book!**" My deepest gratitude and love to *The Ascended Masters in the Heaven World*. They are working diligently to channel the information about the changing consciousness of Humanity, as well as the planetary changes on Mother Earth. They wish to make sure of its availability in language that everyone, from the newly awakening souls, to the most advanced Lightworkers, can understand and resonate to. I wish to thank my dear friend and fellow traveler on the Spiritual Pathway, Sheila Kaplan, for once again accepting to edit my book. Also my special friends Cheri Wolf and Thérèse Denault, for their loving support during this past year. What would I have done without you both!

NOTE TO READERS

I want to share with my readers a little of the *Spiritual phenomena* that took place while writing **The Pathway Home.**

When the channeling began, I had no idea what its title would be. I believed that it would be decided **by a Higher Order.** I was right. While writing the second chapter, the words **The Pathway Home will be the title,** appeared in my mind. As I was preparing the book jacket for printing, I suddenly thought that it would be better to have a sub-title to distinguish **where Home might be.** Immediately, "**A Journey Into Light**" came into my mind.

I awakened one morning, and a painting which seemed to be about eight feet high was standing at the foot of my bed. The vision only lasted about two minutes, but Archangel Michael in all of His Glory was Ascending, holding a child in each arm while others looked on. I knew immediately that this was the painting Spirit wanted on the book jacket. It was the most beautiful sight I had ever seen! The Spiritual energy stayed with me for several days. I met with Ann Marie Eastburn, the wonderful artist who had done the painting for **Soul Rescue**, and described every detail, which had burned itself into my memory.

Channeled through Carole by Mother Mary and St. Joseph, requesting this message to the people of Canada be added to this book.

Mother Mary

I was much venerated by the people in the country you call Canada, the origin of this author. They were like little children, believing in their church teachings, and I held a pious place in their hearts. Many miracles occurred, whether they realized it or not. Their dedication to me as the Mother of the Christ was very deeply imbedded in their souls. Their devotion to Joseph, my beloved husband, to whom they built a shrine, (St.-Joseph Oratory, Montreal, Quebec) in which miracle healings were performed through one of their own, still stands today. The miracles are still happening for the believers.

St.-Joseph

I, too, wish to say a few words to the people of this country. I want them to know that, for those who believe and *have faith that it shall be so,* Divine Healing is as powerful today as it was through my beloved instrument, the one you called *Brother Andre*. We are both still working with all who ask for our help. The *LIGHT* is more powerful at this moment in time than it has ever been in the history of the Planet. Therefore, YOUR FAITH SHALL MAKE YOU WHOLE!

INTRODUCTION

Following the publishing of my first book, *SOUL RESCUE...Help on the Way Home to Spirit*, I had the impression that my next book would be channeled from Spirit. I had no idea what the subject would be, but I knew it would somehow be a continuation of the spiritual teachings I had been sharing over the past fifteen years, to awaken humanity to its divinity.

Over the last two years, through reading a channeling from SANANDA, (who had an incarnation as *Jesus, the Christ*), I had been awakened to the knowledge of the approaching ascension of Mother Earth and all of her inhabitants. This article instantly triggered something in my soul; I spent two days in a state of bliss, sometimes on my knees in prayer for long periods of time. I was never the same again. This was the information I had been awaiting for eons!

I began to realize that many books were being channeled from the Ascended Masters: *Sananda, Count St.-Germain,* Master of the Violet Ray in charge of the transmutation of the planet, *Archangel Gabriel, Archangel Michael,* and many other Ascended Masters.

To give me insight as to my next step, I felt that I needed to consult a good medium for a personal reading. In December, 1993, I found one who channeled the Ascended Masters while in a deep state of trance, which is always what I look for in a medium. It is my belief that the information coming through has less chance of being influenced by the medium's subconscious mind, and is therefore more accurate.

The first spirit who came through to greet me was **EL MORYA, Ascended Master of the First Ray.** He said that **YESHUA**–another of Sananda's incarnations, and about whom books have been written–and **ARCHANGEL GABRIEL** had come with him. At the present time, they were the ones working the closest with my energy.

He asked that I make myself available on a more regular basis throughout the day in the coming months so they could connect with me, and bring through information pertaining to releasing karma and transmuting energies, which would be put in another book.

El Morya said: "You may also find that you are revolving nearer to the Ascended One called **COUNT ST.-GERMAIN** He will vibrate closer to you as the months of the New Year go forward, and you will find that much information will come from this one who is the *Master of the Aquarian Age and the Violet Ray of Transmutation and Releasement*".

"Also know that, at this time, you are writing on the beautiful rays coming from the energy of **El Morya.** The blue emanation, or the blue ray, is allowing you to more fully comprehend the communication skills that you have within you at this time, enabling you to better edit that information which will come through you with greater abundance as time progresses."

I asked him if he could tell me the subject of my next book, and he replied, "There will be much information coming through from the **Realms of the Angelics.** This is why you are drawing close to your friend, **Archangel Gabriel,** as he will be helping you with the communication factors. **Archangel Michael** is also near to you, assisting with the souls making the transition, especially those on the **planes of darkness who are making their transition into the Light.** Information such as this might be appropriate for the next publication."

With three books supposedly being channeled at the same time... I wondered when I was going to have time to sleep. I smiled and said, "I guess you guys forget that those of us still in a human body need to sleep once in awhile, but I'll do my best!"

Over the next few months I was very busy seeing to the editing, professional typesetting and re-publication of *Soul Rescue,* as well as the promotional work for both the English and French version. Occasionally I would take time to channel, and it was always different Ascended Masters giving me information. After reading many of the books on the ascension in the bookstores, some containing very advanced material, I began to compare what I was receiving with what was being channeled through other mediums. I felt that my channelings were very basic material, and wondered why I was not being given more advanced information. Because of my own blockages, I put everything on hold and didn't put any effort into my channeling. My friend Sheila kept telling me that I had to start writing the next book, and finally I realized that I was blocking myself because of my fears of not being worthy. I knew it was time to start, and see what would happen! I promised that I would sit and channel every morning for at least half an hour.

Sananda came through the first day and channeled material which I had felt was basic in the other channelings. Suddenly I realized that what I was receiving was given in a language that newly awakening souls could understand and accept, and would be very important to people who had never heard of the Ascension of Mother Earth. What **Sananda** then conveyed to me was: "That following the publishing of my first book, which would awaken so many souls to their divinity, the readers would be ready for the second one. Therefore, it had to be written in words with which they could identify." In my fifteen years of spiritual work, I have always taken the "Highest Teachings" – Natural, Spiritual and Karmic law – and brought them down to earth, explaining them in a way that everyone could understand. Now I realized that Spirit was making sure that my next book would reach the same type of people, primarily beginners on the spiritual pathway.

What I am sharing with you next is what I consider one of my *most awesome* experiences in the seventeen years I have been working closely with the Spirit World!

During **El Morya's** reading, he told me: "There are some writings of old that you have not looked at in a very long while, as possibly you did not understand them at that time. You might wish to remove these from their storage area and see how you vibrate with them now."

When I recalled his words I tried to imagine what he was talking about! The only thing that came to mind was a book I purchased during my visit to a spiritual center in Florida, in April of 1991.

After returning from a Canadian promotional tour in April 1994, I decided to sit by the water and read for relaxion. I selected a book I hadn't looked at in a long time. Its title was *MAPP* To Aquarius*, one of the books I had bought three years earlier at the Spiritual Center called Mark Age, in Davie, Florida.

Being the *Aries* that I am, a book has to grab my attention and hold it from the beginning, otherwise I will put it aside and most likely never pick it up again. For some unknown reason, I started reading the Introduction, rather than the first chapter, as I usually do.

The book was channeled by the *Spiritual Hierarchy* through Nada-Yolanda. This was the name of the Soul and Higher Self identity divulged to her by the Ascended Masters whom the medium channeled from the beginning of her work in the 1950's. In the introduction, she shared her experiences of how her spiritual work began, and talked about the soul mate that Spirit said would be put on her pathway to help her with a very important mission. They said a scientist would come into her life who would verify the messages.

Under strange circumstances, one day a man did come into her life and they started talking about metaphysics. She said that from their first meeting, she trusted him completely, sensing that he was the most Christlike person she had ever met. Nada-Yolanda and this man whom she called Mark, worked together for many years. Mark verified and edited her channelings, which they published as Spirit had requested.

She went on to say that on April 24, 1981, Mark suddenly passed to Spirit, which was a surprise to them both! From the Spirit World, he has continued directing the Organization of **the I Am Nation.** Near the end of the *Introduction*, she explained that at some point in their work, the Ascended Masters divulged that Mark, as his Higher Self... **was El Morya, Director of the First Ray of Will and Power.**

When I read this, I was in awe at the realization that ***El Morya,*** this Ascended Master who had channeled to me and who had asked me to read a certain book I had not been ready to understand years before, **had, in his last incarnation, lived *a parallel life* in Davie, Florida. The Spirit World explains that our soul is like a diamond, with many facets or prisms and each one is a different part of us that can be evolving in several locations at the same time. We can incarnate on Planet Earth, and at the same time a different facet of our soul is evolving on another planet somewhere in the Universe; or as in El Morya's case, if there is a special mission we need to undertake, we can be living a parallel life in the Spirit World, as well as on Earth.** He had been the **Co-Founder** of the *I Am Nation*, and editor for the channelings from the Ascended Masters brought through Nada-Yolanda at the Mark Age Spiritual Center, which had published that book.

The editing for this second book flowed so well through the beautiful energy of the Blue Ray of *El Morya.* The phrases turned around in my mind and seemed to print themselves on the screen. Since December 1994, I have had three people from different areas, two strangers whom I had never met, ask me if I had ever been to Mark Age, the Spiritual Center in Davie. One invited me to go with her to the meditation they have every Friday night. I have not yet found the time to visit this center again, but I am sure it is a special place where, for some reason, Spirit wants me to go.

Five mornings in a row, **Sananda, Archangel Gabriel, St.-Germain, Serapis Bey,** (another Ascended Master who is playing an important role in the ascension of Mother Earth) and ***Archangel Michael*** took turns channeling important information. I realized the many long hours of work it would take to transcribe the tapes, and put them on my computer. I asked if it would be possible for them to channel directly to me while I was sitting at the computer, and they said it could be done. We had a couple of practice sessions, and the information started to flow directly into my mind, which I put on the computer phrase by phrase. ***This is the way most of this book was channeled!***

***MY WISH FOR EACH OF YOU, IS THAT YOU HAVE
A MARVELOUS JOURNEY ON***

YOUR PATHWAY HOME.

I Love You!
    Carole

CHAPTER ONE

ENDINGS AND NEW BEGINNINGS

We are living in extraordinary times, my friends! Many strange things are happening on our planet; at least they may seem *strange* or *unusual* to many of us. But this is all part of the Divine plan of the Father/Mother God, Creator of The All That Is, for the ascension of Planet Earth when the time is right.

The preparations have been underway for eons, and the plan has been followed one step at a time, as it was meant to be. Now is a very important moment for Planet Earth, which is going into a new dimension along with all of her inhabitants. You shall be hearing more and more about the word *ascension* in the near future.

The planet has been surrounded with spiritual energy in preparation for Mother Earth taking her final step. Our way of thinking is changing and many are helping diligently by projecting loving energy for healing, knowing that she is suffering greatly at this moment in time. They are working with the oceans, the seas, the sky and the earth. Some are working with the animals, trying to save many species which are disappearing from the planet.

The knowledge that you have inside is coming to the forefront at this time. This inner knowledge is very precious. Bring it out and let it flow into your mind, then down through your heart, to process it. You are not all at the same point of evolution, and for some it will take a longer period of time. Take only the information that is comfortable for you, and stay open on the rest.

The souls who are awakening to their true identities will stand tall and take responsibility for what and whom they are, as they recognize themselves and each other. As you go down that new pathway, many new doors will open for you. People who are of like mind and with loving hearts shall be put on your pathway, and you must support and help each other in your spiritual growth.

The love will be very powerful, and the true healings will begin working through the heart chakra. The power of love is the most important thing that exists at this moment; it is even stronger than the Light, and we must learn to love ourselves as much as God loves us. Accept who you are, and appreciate how far you have come. Never compare yourself with another; just open and awaken, and let your beloved spirit guides assist you in unfolding your spiritual gifts.

It is important that you join others of like mind to sit in a spiritual development group to reinforce the power of the energy. It is also imperative that the leader of your group have the knowledge to lead you gently into your awakening and the development of your spiritual gifts. You must have full confidence in this person, as you release all fear and open yourself to universal energy, knowing that you are always fully protected.

As the awakening begins, you will look back and see what you considered *coincidences* in your life that have brought you to the point where you are now. For a long time your guides have been gently *nudging* you to move forward on your pathway.

Spiritual gifts can be varied, depending on past life experiences. Sometimes we spent many lifetimes specializing in one gift such as healing, perfecting the different techniques used at that time, and succeeded in reinforcing our power to perform what some called ***miracle*** healing. Many others, like myself, are blessed with several gifts and have come in at this time to work in many spiritual areas. During past lives regression sessions and readings through deep trance mediums, I have learned of many lifetimes I have had – one as a North American Indian, living in the area where the city of Toronto, Ontario is today. I was told that I was a **Shaman,** but was not permitted to have the title during that incarnation because I was a woman. Tribes came to me for healing from all around the country. I also had another incarnation as a Shaman in the area where the Hawaiian Islands are today. A young man, one of my students in this lifetime, was my younger brother in that period. I taught him healing in that lifetime also. For what I feel will be my last incarnation on Planet Earth, I have so much to do that it seems they gave me the ***whole package:*** discernment of spirits, (now known on the planet as mediumship), clairvoyance, healing, and teaching the Natural, Spiritual and Karmic Laws, which I supposedly learned in a lifetime two thousand years ago. All of this, in addition to the writing of several books to awaken humanity to its Divinity, and to help in the preparation of the ascension of the planet! It is **no wonder, astrologically speaking, I incarnated this time with a *double fire sign,* (Aries with a Sagittarius ascendant), and four planets in Virgo!**

I realize that I am truly blessed to have been given so many spiritual gifts, but at times the responsibility to live up to the Spirit World's expectation of me weighs heavily on my heart. The difficult moments in my life when I was working out my own karmic patterns, were often emotionally devastating to me. If these situations continued for an extended period of time, they always ended in physical problems which took time to heal. Because I couldn't seem to deal on a spiritual level with everything in my material and physical life, I often feared that my guides would be disappointed in me. It is in understanding that our soul must manifest within the confines of our physical body that we can accept our limits. Only then can we forgive ourselves, and know that what we consider to be a weakness is part of our humanness, as well as the working out of the last of our karma.

Without the physical body, we could not accomplish our mission. Our beloved guides and Masters understand this, and are patient with us; but it is now time for us to move forward on the spiritual path of self-realization, with full awakening and remembrance of who we are as the soul. While in the World of Spirit before incarnating, we accepted an assignment and made a covenant with the Father/Mother God. *Now we must fulfill our promise, move forward and take our rightful place as a Lightworker.*

Over our many lifetimes on the planet, we forgot that *we were Spiritual beings having a human experience in a physical body.* Little by little, we gave away our power. Now it is time to take back that power!

Our power is derived from the understanding of the Natural and Spiritual Laws of the Universe. First, we must love ourselves as much as God loves us. This will give us the sense of value that we need to function in a physical world full of selfishness. Most humans do not know how to love themselves or others. Therefore, there are many destructive patterns in our world today that must be reversed.

If we know who we truly are, beloved children of God who have been blessed by having been permitted to attain soul growth through an earthly incarnation, we see life very differently. We recognize each experience as an opportunity to **advance** or **regress,** in our soul growth; it is our choice. When we finally understand and accept that there is a reason for everything that happens in our lives, that *an accident or coincidence does not exist,* we will take a quantum leap forward into our spiritual understanding of the *Natural Law of Cause and Effect.*

Through their channelings to evolved spiritual groups in many parts of the world over the past few years, the Ascended Masters have been preparing us for the changes that will take place in our personal lives, as well as on a global level.

They told us: *"Karma, as you now understand it, will be finished on the planet in 1995".* This meant that in every area of our lives, whatever we had to resolve on a karmic level would soon be terminated. This is why we were going through so much unrest in our personal lives over the last few years; our souls were telling us that it was time to make some changes in many situations – personal as well as careerwise.

Unbeknown to us on a conscious level, our souls were trying to help us understand that **school was over,** and we would soon be graduating. *God's experimentation on His beautiful Planet Earth for millions of years was ending;* all his beloved children would finally be returning *Home!*

In preparation for this, many changes had to take place; first and foremost on a spiritual level. There had to be a massive awakening of Humanity to its Divinity! Once the soul was awakened, it would take its rightful place in the seeker's life, and try to lead them onto the pathway it had chosen before its incarnation.

Through the **Quantum Leap** that mankind has taken following the elevation of the vibratory rate on the planet over the past few years, millions have had an awakening of one kind or another. When one partner awakened first and began to move onto the spiritual pathway, it was often difficult, especially for a couple who had been together for many years! To see the changes in their loved one's perception of life, and not comprehending what was taking place, often caused dissension in the family. The soul, which was finally ready to take its rightful place in the Universe and complete its Divine pattern, would no longer accept someone else dominating its life; thus began the sometimes long and rocky road to **Taking Back Our Power!**

We must **allow ourselves and others** the freedom to complete the pattern we chose before incarnating. If we permit them to do so, the Spirit World will influence our lives and turn us in the direction of our chosen path. As the awakening takes place and new doors open, we will be put in situations... and the right people with whom we are to do our work will appear in our lives.

Now is the time when the *spiritual families* will be finding each other on the planet and begin the work they chose to do before incarnating. We sometimes meet someone for the first time, and feel as if we have known them forever. This is because we have spent many incarnations together. Often we have evolved our spiritual gifts in the same areas on the planet in those lifetimes. Now, following the **Awakening of Humanity to its Divinity**, we are back for the *Grand Finale.*

Once we begin to understand and accept who we are and what we came to do, our evolution proceeds at a quickened pace. It is very important to have a loving support group in the spiritual field. Often there comes a time when we think that our Earth families don't understand us, and we are devastated by their rejection of our new way of thinking. We must remember that those who have never learned to love themselves feel the need to control; this is the way they have always found their sense of value. When they realize they can no longer control their partner in life, or a child who has grown in wisdom and awakened to its Divine heritage, they will do all they can to prevent what they perceive as **losing them**. They will try ridicule, intimidation, and sometimes tears if all else fails!

We must understand that we are all instruments for each other's growth; that possibly the lesson we came to help them learn is to release their fears. Fears of many kinds–rejection, of not being loved, or not living up to others expectations of us – have kept us prisoners of ourselves over many lifetimes. As we finish up our karma, we need to release these fears so that we may be whole once again, that we may understand our true place in the scheme of the **Divine Plan, which is the return of all the Earth children to our Heavenly Home with complete remembrance of who we are as the soul.**

Through finding our own center of inner peace, and becoming a living example of unconditional love for every living thing on this planet, they may be influenced and helped in their awakening. As a flower opens to the sun, each new day will be more fulfilling than the one before!

We try to work through the conflicts involved when two personalities no longer have a meeting of minds, but often this brings a couple to the parting of the ways. On a karmic level, each has learned all he can from this relationship. If they both realize that the love they once had for each other has gone from their union, it is time to make decisions as to what would be the

highest good and the greatest growth potential of everyone involved.

It must be done in a loving way. The emotional pain is very deep, not only for the one left behind, but also for the one who made the decision to begin a new life elsewhere. The one leaving always has to work out a sense of guilt, while the one who is left behind feels rejected, and often pride takes over! They function from the ego for a long period of time, until the pain subsides and they start to come out of their depressed state. Everyone acquires soul growth through these experiences if they will permit themselves to do so; and there will come a time when they realize that what happened was for the best for all concerned.

When there are children involved it is imperative that they be traumatized as little as possible. **Because they chose you as parents** before incarnating, the souls in these little beings knew the experiences they would be going through, but on a conscious level they do not remember this. For the love of the children, we must keep their small world as normal as possible while we are going through all the upheavals a separation entails. We must help them to understand that both parents still love them very much, and what is happening has nothing to do with them. It has been proven that children feel a sense of guilt, that somehow it is their fault that Mommy and Daddy are not living in the same house anymore. They must be made to understand that they are equally loved by both parents, and that they will always be there for them and continue to play an important role in their lives.

Many of the children who have been born over the past few years are special, and have incarnated with no karma to work out. Some have chosen to be here to help their father and mother go through the traumatic period that, soulwise, these little ones knew they would be facing at this point in their lives.

Whatever happens, if you feel that you are experiencing the most devastating situation of your life, it is important that you remember that you are never alone. There are wonderful therapists, and loving organizations out there to help you work through the trauma. If you try to understand what is happening, why your world seems to have fallen apart, it is important to look within yourselves for the answers – then ask for Divine help. The God of your own understanding is always there for you, and He loves you; you are unique and special in His eyes. Ask for His help, and the sense of inner peace you will have following this conversation will be like nothing you have ever felt before. You will know that God and His messengers, our beloved guardian angels, have always been close to us, but we didn't open the door and invite them in! Because we always had *free will*, they could only wait for an invitation.

My dear friends, as you work through each **wonderful lesson in soul growth** – they are really blessings in disguise – remember and keep repeating one phrase which will give you the strength to come through these times: *"This too shall pass!"* Following acceptance, you will become much stronger, and will look forward to starting a new life.

CHAPTER TWO

RELEASING THE DENSITY

As the preparation for the changes occurring on the planet go forward, there are many changes that must take place inside ourselves. These changes must come from the inside before they can manifest in our physical life.

There is much inner self work to be done in the area of letting go of the ego and allowing our Higher Self to direct our lives. We must release the pride, and learn to be humble through the understanding that all spiritual gifts come from God; **of ourselves, we are nothing**!

First humanity must learn to love itself. We always functioned from the ego, and were taught that thinking of ourselves first was a very selfish attitude to have. We didn't understand that when Jesus said, "**Love thy neighbor *as* thyself**", that was exactly what He meant. If we are always giving, and are unable to receive because subconsciously we feel we are not worthy, there is no balance in our life where **the Natural Law of Giving and Receiving** is concerned.

Subconsciously, we always felt unworthy and guilty, even though we didn't understand where these feelings were coming from. Much of this was caused by the unconscious memory of our **Fall from Grace**. At some point in our evolution we chose Earthly pleasures over our Divine Heritage, and moved away from God.

By learning to love ourselves, we will finally understand what Jesus meant two thousand years ago when He brought this message to us in His teachings. We lived many incarnations over thousands of years, trying to get this lesson straight, but few really understood. This was one of the most important lessons Christ brought to us when He took on physical form in His incarnation as Jesus the Christ, and was considered to be **one of the most important events in the history of Humanity.**

He considered this part of His teachings so important because He knew that once we had understood it our whole life would change. By loving ourselves we connect with our Higher Self, and allow it to direct our lives. When we have decisions to make, we will listen to the still small voice telling us what experiences are for our highest good, or for the highest good of another who might be involved. We are often used as instruments to help others evolve soulwise, and sometimes this means saying "*no*". Many times, our soul tried to warn through a certain feeling in the solar plexus, that the decision our mind was about to make was incorrect; but still we didn't listen! It was only later that we would usually admit to a friend: "My gut feeling told me not to do this, but I didn't listen!"

When we learn to love ourselves, we bring a sense of balance to our inner being, filling our heart with joy. We wake up in the morning with a song in our heart, and the music plays all day long if we don't allow life's lessons to bring down our light. There are two ways to see each experience in our life–negative or positive. By our perception of the situation, we have the choice to accept whichever energy we wish. By understanding the concept that there is a lesson to learn from whatever is happening, we can *refuse* to accept negativity of any kind in our life and ask our Higher Self what this lesson is.

Releasing the Density ~41

If we allow a negative reaction to enter our vibration, we start a chain of events that may take a while to work themselves out. Remember... ***all illness is self inflicted!*** If we stay in the negative energy for a long period of time through wrong attitudes, we may also create an effect in our physical body; remember the headaches, etc. you gave yourself when you worried over situations in your life? Because of karma having terminated on the planet in 1995, we are no longer paying for mistakes made in past incarnations. Therefore situations can only be created through **cause and effect direct:** ***your thoughts today, is your reality tomorrow!***

There is no longer a need for us to have anything but perfect health. There is a reason for every illness, and a lesson to be learned from it. Through the understanding of the termination of karma on Earth, we need to tune into our Higher Selves to find out why this **dis-ease** is still in our body... why it is still needed in our life? What is the lesson we have not heeded?

First, I believe we have to learn to connect with our physical body, and tell each part how much we appreciate it functioning perfectly, year in and year out. We always took our vehicle for granted, expecting it to work diligently for all the time we needed to manifest through it. It often took our selfish actions and abuse until different parts of the body were damaged or worn out, and had to be surgically removed. This perfect vehicle was made to last for hundreds of years, if we had learned to care, nurture and love it the way we should have.

Our body can channel its needs to us. We only have to sit quietly, tune into it, and ask if there is anything it needs that it is not receiving. You will be very surprised to hear an answer pop into your mind, or receive a picture of a certain fruit, vegetable or other food. You may even hear the name of a vitamin or mineral that it is lacking. It can become so proficient at expressing its needs, that it can also tell you how many of these pills it needs each day, and for how long a period necessary to bring it back to perfect health.

It is important to become conscious of what we have done, and take responsibility by trying to make amends. Take some time each day to turn your thoughts towards the care of your body, by consciously sending love to every part of it. This simple exercise, done two or three times a week, will help you bring health and balance into every part of your physical body.

****

Lie on the floor or on a bed! Breathe deeply and gently, until you feel your body completely relaxed and centered from head to foot. Starting at the top of your head, lay your hand or hands – you can do both sides at the same time – on each part of this beautiful vehicle, one area at a time. Breathe deeply, and with each exhalation visualize and feel pink light flowing from your heart, through your arms and hands, directly into that area. As you move to each part of your body, you will begin to sense a feeling of excitement. It will feel the love vibration flowing to it, possibly for the first time in its existence. If your sensitivity is highly developed, you may feel it vibrating in a more balanced way. The parts that need the most attention are the ones you possibly disliked the most over your lifetime. Give special loving attention to the inner organs – the ones for which you probably had the greatest disdain. Without their important eliminatory function, your body could not have survived. Continue projecting until you feel the body glowing from the love it is receiving.

If you had prior problems in certain areas, such as blood pressure, heart rhythm, etc., this self healing body meditation may possibly result in an improvement in the condition.

****

As you begin to clear the past to move onto your new pathway, much will surface to be cleared and released. It is important to put some order in what in being revealed, and the reason why it is surfacing at this moment in time. Experiences from all of your lifetimes, both positive and negative lie dormant in your subconscious mind. It is important to call on St. Germain, who is in charge of the transmutation on the planet through the energy of the *violet light and violet flame*. Every situation in our lives and on the planet needs to be surrounded with this powerful Ray to transmute everything that is not of the highest order. You may call on the violet light to transmute any negative thought that comes into your mind, and it will disappear immediately, leaving you serene once again. This may also be of a physical nature, some condition that you had in a previous incarnation which is still there on a cellular level.

If you have difficulty releasing all the old *stuff* you have held in your vibration for eons, request help from your guides or guardian angels. They will put someone on your pathway to help you. No request for help sent up into the ethers remains unanswered, especially where the awakening Lightworkers are concerned; but you must ask. For those of you who wish to clear this past life residue quickly, there are Lightworkers in alternative medicines who specialize in the new techniques of releasing at a cellular level. You will be surprised at what you might consider a series of coincidences, that will put the right person on your path. But *know* that an accident or a coincidence doesn't exist... everything is **synchronicity.**

As you start meditating on a regular basis, you will become more familiar with your beloved guides, who have possibly worked with you in many lifetimes. As you learn to meditate on a deeper level, you will begin to sense their presence each time they come close to you. You may get a feeling of someone standing behind you and gently putting their hand on your shoulder; or you may sense a gentle loving touch, as if someone were laying a hand on your head giving you a blessing. As your gifts begin to unfold, there will possibly be several guides working with you, each with his own specialty. Request their names, and if you cannot psychically receive it, ask that they appear to you in the dream state and identify themselves.

If you sincerely desire to progress in the development of your spiritual gifts, it is important that you respect your guides, and always sit for your meditations at the same time each day. If you are delayed or cannot sit at your usual time, send up a thought during the day to your guide, advising him of this. A gesture such as this will make him realize that you are a thoughtful, loving being, and he will be very loyal to you in return. Each guide is working with many souls. If they know that you will be there at the same time on a regular basis, they will always be there, waiting to take you further in your growth. The more you open and trust, the faster you will begin the important work you came to do in this incarnation.

Now that you have released the ego and are working through your Higher Self, it is important to have pride in your work, yet stay humble. All of this blessed work, sometimes even miracles, comes *through us*... but it is coming from the God energy. If we misuse the **power,** the spiritual gifts can be taken from us. People recognize those who say they are doing God's work, but *take the glory for themselves* because the ego is still very strong in them. This will no longer be acceptable, as an awakening humanity is looking more and more for those of a spiritual nature to help in their healing.

The time for the separation between the World of Spirit and the children of Earth is over. We are coming into full realization of who we are as the soul, and it is time to reconnect with our Real Home in the Spirit World .

As you follow your spiritual path and commence the important work your soul chose to do, you need to sensitize yourself to Spirit. Even though it is important to stay grounded most of the time, it is imperative that your guides be able to reach you if there is something important they think you need to know, or if they wish to use you as an instrument to help others.

We can stay grounded, doing our Earthly work, but still have our *feelers* out for anyone who may need help on some level. When we see or sense that someone is in emotional turmoil, we need to surround them with loving thoughts. Often they are trying to deal with something on a personal level which is devastating to them, but which they are trying to hide. A friendly word, or a loving pat on the shoulder to let them know **someone cares,** is a very important gesture to make. So many people are going through their own personal hell and don't know where to turn for help. They feel that they are alone in their pain, and their fear or pride prevents them from sharing their experience with others. A Spiritual guide, or sometimes even a family member who has passed to spirit, will influence us to gently intervene, and to at least give them moral support by allowing them to open their heart and share their problem. By knowing they have someone impartial with whom to talk, an inner healing and balance begins immediately. It is the feeling of being completely alone that is devastating to body, mind, and spirit. Let them share their thoughts and solutions for the problem with you, but never make the decisions for them.

If you are a healer, you may suddenly sense that someone you know needs a healing, and you will possibly also sense in which area of the body the problem lies. If you can, sit quietly and go into your altered state of consciousness. Project yourself to them through your Astral or Light body, and do the healing. If you are in a place where it is impossible to properly project yourself, at least send mental healing and call on the healing forces who work with you, to go to them.

Remember that we are channels and must use our healing energy, whether it be for mental, emotional or physical healing. With past life karma having terminated on the planet, we may now send out the healing energy to anyone we wish to help. Project to anyone who needs it, and if on some level of their being they request a healing, they will receive it. When you finish your meditation and healing sessions each day, surround Mother Earth with the colors pink for love, and blue for healing. She will greatly appreciate this and will bless you for it.

As you become more and more aware of the changes in the energy field and the speeding up of time on the planet, you will realize that something is happening all over the globe, of which we have no control. We are noticing the changes in the weather patterns, with more earthquakes, tornadoes etc., along with dry spells or periods of heavy rain that destroy the crops in many parts of the world.

We are allowing more fear to enter our consciousness, worrying about where all these devastating occurrences will take us. We need to go back to praying to the God of our own understanding, and learn to meditate. Prayer changes our whole outlook on any situation, as we feel that we are no longer alone... that we have the highest power in the Universe walking by our side, and have a direct connection at all times. We will become so balanced in our faith that we will *know in the very core of our being,* that whatever happens will be in Divine Order. We need to ask our guardian angels to stay close to us in case we need their help. *Knowing* that we are always Divinely protected helps us to get on with the rest of our earthly life, enjoying this beautiful planet which has been our temporary home over so many lifetimes.

As you walk tall with unshakable faith that the Spiritual Beings in the Heaven World are walking by your side, you will begin to have flashes of remembrance of your life in that world between Earthly incarnations, and great joy will fill your heart.

As you spend more time connected to the Spirit World, situations around you that were not for your highest good will be cleared in one way or another. At first you may not realize what is happening; then one day you begin to notice that everything in your life is moving forward with greater balance and clarity. Those on Earth who are part of your spiritual family, and with whom you have a strong soul connection, will be moving onto your pathway. They will be gently eased into your life pattern without your really taking steps for this to happen. When you meet for the first time, you will have an instant feeling of having always known them. You have had many incarnations together on Planet Earth and are back for the *finale,* as you prepare yourself for your imminent ascension along with Mother Earth.

CHAPTER THREE

PATHWAY TO ASCENSION

SANANDA

From the beginning of time, the Father/Mother/Creator's plan for Planet Earth was to give the inhabitants free will; the souls that incarnated on Mother Earth would have the right to make their own decisions. The Law of Cause and Effect was implemented at that time, and has continued since that moment. This was a new process with which God wanted to experiment on this unique planet. He wanted to see what His children, who came to Earth in their light bodies for the first time, would do when they came in contact with both positive and negative energies, and had choices to make. They had never known that the negative even existed! Through the Law of Cause and Effect, their choices would affect their soul growth. Thus began the eternal **wheel of karma,** where each soul returned over and over to make retribution to other souls for the pain they had caused them. A balance had to be brought forth in one lifetime or another.

At the beginning it was very simple for them because they were used to their life and their light in the spirit world; but as the density of the energy on the planet intensified, the changes, which were following the pattern of the energy, began to manifest in their light bodies. They were taking on the density of the Earth energy through the thought process – **as you think, so you are**. As times changed, humanity took steps towards the negative energy, which they should not have done; this changed everything in the area of the universe where they now abided. They came to enjoy the pleasures of this wonderful planet, and many of them forgot that their real Home was in the Spirit World.

At the beginning, they would go back and forth to the World of Spirit, the place they knew as Home; but later on, they enjoyed the planet so much that they went back less and less. Finally there came a time when they would only return Home for a short visit.

Do remember that this planet is unique, dear children; there is not another like it in all the universes. You were privileged to have been permitted to come to experience and experiment with *time,* which does not exist anywhere else in the universe, and to be subject to the **Law of Cause and Effect** and *free will.* You returned over and over, because you chose to come back for the growth of the soul. This was the unique reason Planet Earth was given free will – this was the place the souls could acquire the most soul growth.

As you approach the time for the Ascension, you will begin to sense this inner feeling that **something different is happening out there!** By trying to understand yourself as a human being, you will begin to realize that there is a part of you missing, that your human side is not all there is. There is a part of you which is yearning for something... but you know not what. You continue the search for the missing piece, and a door opens in your awakening consciousness. Someone will be put on your pathway to help you to realize who you are as the soul, and what you came to do in this last incarnation.

Your beloved guides and guardian angels have always been there for you, since the first moment you incarnated on the planet. They have never forsaken you, but you forgot about them – who they were and why they were there. They were waiting for you to ask for their help.

Many of the souls on Earth are beginning to realize that the Beings in the Angelic kingdom are drawing closer to them. They are drawing closer to you, dear children, because you are drawing nearer to them through the releasing of the density of the energy on the planet and the awakening of your souls. This is opening doors to a new way of thinking, new energies and possibilities you would never have dreamed of twenty years ago... for some of you, even two years ago!

Very soon, most of you will have the awakening necessary to prepare for the return to the Spirit World through the ascension of Mother Earth. The reality is that She has finished playing her part in the Divine plan created eons ago, and is now returning to the fifth dimension from where She originally came. The cleansing and balancing shall take place, but the devastation will not be as much as prophesied over hundreds of years. Mankind has awakened faster than even we in the Spirit World who are in charge of this project expected, or ever dreamed possible.

We want you to know that as of this month, (October 1994), Mother Earth will have taken a quantum leap in her growth and in her ascension. Along with her shall be Mankind, taking a giant step in its **faith**!

Because of the higher vibrations, many changes will take place in each of your lives. Some that are more aware may expect to have Spiritual visions. Wonderful people will be put on your pathway to open the doors that have not yet opened because of the dense energy in your physical bodies and in your minds. You will realize within a few days that the energies around you will have dramatically changed... they will seem so much lighter. You will feel as if something has changed. The air that you breath will be vibrating so fast, that those of you who are sensitive will feel your physical bodies vibrating with this energy. It is as if your feet were lifting off the ground.

You are able to sense when important changes are made as the Spirit World anchors the new energy on the planet, taking quantum leaps in every area. This is a very important step to help humanity as it moves towards the next dimension.

We know that you shall feel these new energies, and that you will take the necessary steps to make the changes needed in your own lives. It is also a time for releasing, a time for detachment from the situations and things in your lives that don't seem as important as they once were, because they no longer serve you on a karmic level.

The karmic patterns you had to work out are ending! You will know in the very depths of your soul what situations we are talking about. Each one is being brought to the surface to be cleared, cleansed, and for the Light to be put on it. Mother Earth is ascending and Her beloved children are ascending along with her.

We will be teaching you the important things you need to know about releasing the density. You may prepare your own energy by elevating your vibrations through meditation techniques. By constant practice, your light body will connect with your physical body. In time the two will merge and move forward, with the light body taking control for longer periods of time. There will come a time when you will be able to go back and forth at will to both dimensions.

As you begin the cleansing process from the subconscious mind, more and more "**stuff**" will surface for you to face. *Know* that nothing from the past can touch you, unless you allow it to do so by hanging on to a memory that no longer serves you. It was all a part of your learning lessons in this last incarnation on Planet Earth, the time when all the children on the planet must remember who they truly are.

Every negative situation in your lives which you are clinging to for one reason or another, must be released!. You may want to punish someone by refusing to forgive and forget, continually using the **guilt trip as your method of punishment.** You want to see them as unhappy as you feel they have made you. Please understand that karmic lessons were working out in each situation, and much soul growth was possible if you worked through it. You all had choices to make, whether to allow someone else to control your life or, by going through devastating experiences, learn to take back your power. Before incarnating, you chose whatever situations you had to work through in this lifetime. Your soul needed this experience for its growth, or was instrumental in the soul growth of others. When you learn to accept the true concept of karma, you will be able to close the door on negativity in this lifetime, understanding that whatever happened was the choice of your soul for its evolution, and was for your highest good!

Do not fear what is coming, dear children of Earth; you are all protected. As you know... ***There is no death!*** There never has been. As the souls awaken more and more in preparation for the ascension by allowing their light bodies to take their proper place in their lives, all fear shall dissipate. You will finally realize who you are as the soul. We are close to each and every one who will open his heart and permit us to enter, and help you to understand what is coming forth from the Light.

Release all the fears and mental anguish! Clear and cleanse the emotional body, releasing the residue of all your karmic lifetimes... let them go. Release the negativity... release the fears. There is no reason to fear, dear ones, except in your mind. The fears are surfacing from your subconscious to be recognized, acknowledged and released. As a fear comes forth to be put into the light, acknowledge it, give it love and let it go. Each fear that you release will disappear forever unless you reclaim it by bringing it to the surface once again to reexamine, as the earth children are prone to do. They are finished... do not bring them back! You can finally let go of all these negative experiences in your lives, because as light beings, they are no longer of any use to you. Bless them for being a part of your lessons, and release them with love. See them ascending into the light, and we promise you they shall not return.

We ask that you do this on a daily basis and in a short time you shall see the changes in your bodies. Your emotional body will be much more balanced, and your physical body will finally let go of the density which it has held each Earthly lifetime. By practicing during your meditations you will soon realize that your light bodies are merging with your physical bodies. You will be working more and more through your light bodies. Your **Light** will become so bright that you will be a catalyst to help others change without their even knowing that you are doing so, **because you *ARE* Light,** beloved children, never forget this! You have *always been Light*... but you fell asleep and forgot. Now is the time for the **awakening!** The awakening into a new world of beauty, love, peace and joy like you have never known. Through the suffering in your Earthly incarnations, you received immense growth. Each time, you made the choice to return to this planet to erase and balance the mistakes you had made in the previous lifetime. As you begin to understand this process, you will release all of the negativity, finally accepting that everything in your lives happened for one reason only... ***the growth of the soul.***

We are close to you with our spaceships, but we are in a different dimension. You can only connect with us if you go into an altered state of consciousness. We want to assure you that there is no danger for you. Everything is in Divine Order and, as the vibrations accelerate and the Light is put stronger around the planet, everything will unfold exactly as it has been pre-ordained. We are there for you... you only have to send out a thought. The destruction you had feared for so long will not be as drastic as expected, because you are changing. Your beloved Mother Earth must do Her cleansing and healing before she can fully ascend. She will reverse the destruction, and release the negativity and stress mankind has put on Her over eons through their wrong attitudes, selfishness and greed. They refused to realize that without her, humanity could not survive.

We know that many of you have preconceived ideas of what will happen – you have been imbedded with thoughts of fear and destruction of all kinds. Much of what to expect has been given through the teachings of the churches. We ask that you stay open on all of this information; do not take it as the complete truth, because many changes have taken place... and many more, of which they are unaware, are to take place. Mother Earth will do Her cleansing in Her own way, but do know that the destruction shall not be as devastating as prophesied.

Therefore do not worry about anything; know that you have the Highest Commanders in our world in charge of every step of the Ascension of Planet Earth, and it is important that you put your fears aside and learn to flow with the new ***Light*** energy that is there for you.

We ask that you open your hearts and let us in; that you open your hearts and love each other, that each race and creed on the planet may become brothers and sisters in Light, as you originally were. There is no color... there is no race... there is no creed! There is only **Love and Light;** beings of Light who forgot who they were, but you shall return very soon to the remembrance of who you are as the soul.

Do not worry about the fighting and the wars that are taking place... everything is evolving as it should in the process of the cleansing and the clearing, so that mankind may realize how much havoc and devastation they have wreaked with their physical energy and through their thought process. They have brought this on themselves. All the negative thoughts and deeds of humanity over the millions of years have finally come to a head. These are the final effects of the lack of sowing love in their lives and through their thoughts.

We are very close to help you with your awakening. We are with each and everyone of you, to support and aid you in your preparation for the most important event in the history of mankind on the planet, **The Ascension of Mother Earth and all of Her children**. This will take place in peace and joy and love and light, as Mother Earth prepares to take Her final step. She is returning to take Her rightful place in the Universes as the star She originally was, and we are happy for Her. After eons, She will be able to release Her suffering and be Herself again, radiant in all of Her beauty and splendor, with love flowing from Her as it was in the beginning and shall be evermore.

We want you to know that much of the information which has been given concerning the ascension process is correct. There is more than one way in which this can be done. It can be done through your soul awakening, and your taking responsibility on your own through techniques learned from books. It can also be done by several people joining together to empower themselves through group energy. There are also Lightworkers who can help you evolve more quickly in your process by reconnecting your missing DNA strands, and activating your Lightbody.

In the beginning there was more than one plan for saving the planet, dear children; but as humanity awakened spiritually, we devised a plan which would be better and much quicker than the original one which had been planned hundreds of years ago when humanity had not yet awakened.

We are sure that many of you will be able to understand and accept what I am telling you, because your soul knows that this is truth. It is truth that has been laying dormant until the moment of awakening, when this was scheduled to take place. We are happy to say that we are even ahead of the time frame that was foreseen at the beginning.

With all of the negativy on the planet, you may think that the **dark side** is gaining power! This is not true. The souls are awakening and changing, and their new spirituality is elevating the energy on the planet. This will help others to remember who they truly are, and accept that their ascension is imminent. We cannot give you an exact time frame at this moment as we ourselves do not have this knowledge. All depends on how quickly the masses awaken and raise their vibrations, which elevates those of the entire planet.

The energy which is being projected from our side and from other planets, to help in the awakening and the ascension, is of a very high vibratory rate. This has been done through a quickening process... the speeding up of the vibrations so that mankind's energy field will accelerate, and can be felt in their physical bodies. Do not worry, all will be well, and each phase will have an important timing aspect.

You are all awakening to these new energies. Many only realize that time as they know it has speeded up, and a day seems to have a much shorter time span than even a few years ago. There are many questions in their minds, such as what is happening, and the possible reasons for the negativity on the planet. Many are experiencing devastating occurrences in their lives and being taken to the depths of despair for the lessons needed by the soul.

It is very important that you help the newly awakening to understand that this will only accelerate. Everything is being brought to the surface for the light in every area of the planet to be put on it; nothing can remain hidden any longer.

It is normal that there is much worry amongst the people of Earth. They see the violence that is out there, and do not understand that behind this violence is the Light, which is being brought around the situation to transmute it. We realize that the violence is destructive to everybody's lives, but there is a reason for this. It is important that you release all fears and **keep yourselves permanently surrounded in Light,** *because fears are of the darkness, and cannot abide in the same house with love*. Call on us for protection and you shall have it.

Greed among the people of Earth will also change. You will find that there will be scandals in every area and in all endeavors on the planet. In all sections of Government, business, churches and schools etc. **Nothing can remain hidden any longer; all is surfacing for the Light to be put on it.** If you hear of a devastating experience occurring on the planet, know that there is a great lesson being brought forth so that mankind can learn. Sometimes it is to help you realize how low the human race has fallen. Just put the **light and love** around the souls who will be passing back to the Spirit World. Remember that they chose to return in this way, being used as an instrument to help the soul growth for many on the planet. Put everything in perspective in your own lives. It will allow you to understand more clearly what is happening, and enable you to help large groups of souls who are leaving their body at this time, find their way to the Light.

We thank you for permitting us to share this information with you, and we know that it shall be used to help your brothers and sisters on the planet. Do know that more will be brought to you as your awakening accelerates. When we think that humanity is ready to receive and understand important knowledge, we will see that it is relayed to you through one channel or another.

I, Sananda, in the name of the Father/Mother God, bless you for the work you are doing. We are very happy that many are finally awakening and seeing the Light. You will be the Lightworkers who will go forth and open the doors to the non-believers, helping them understand. By **living** your spiritual beliefs and putting them in practice in every situation in your lives, the loving energy will radiate from your aura. Each of you will be recognized as **a human being who has spiritually awakened,** and is living his/her Divinity, helping to raise the vibrations of the planet.

The energy field around Mother Earth will become lighter and more spiritual, providing a quicker release of the density, negativity, and energy of violence that is still held in the Ethers around the planet. Through this process, as more and more of you awaken, there cannot be any other result but the planet's ascension, and your own ascension as well. **We will be waiting to welcome you Home.** *We Bless You!*

CHAPTER FOUR

TRANSFORMATIONS

ST.-GERMAIN

We are coming from a different world than yours, therefore some things we say may be hard for you to understand; but please give credence to what we are saying to you.

The times of endings and new beginnings are here! As you have noticed the changes taking place on the planet, you have been wondering where all these upheavals will take you. Much fear has entered into the minds of the earth children and we understand this, as many devastating things are happening all around them. There will come a time when you will feel that you are standing completely alone, and wonder to whom you can turn for help. It is at this moment that the awakening really begins!

You touch bottom following an upheaval in your personal lives and realize you have no one to turn to for help. Everyone around you seems to be going through the same trauma. This is the moment when you will remember that ***the only person left to whom you can turn is God***. The memories of your childhood, when this *far off personage* held a very special place in your lives, seem to flood back into your memory, and your heart begins to open once again. Your cry for help is all the Heaven World has been waiting for... you are finally admitting that you are nothing without God in your life.

The inner door to your heart, which has been closed for so long, finally opens to the Light which has always been there.

Often it is like a dam breaking. Tears of joy begin to fall, as you realize that you were never forsaken... that **YOU** turned your back on the One who should have held the most important place in your life – *your Creator, Father/Mother God*. He/She was always there for you, but somewhere along your life path you forgot to give God the glory for everything that was happening in your life. Sometimes it was through your upbringing, when your parents were not close to God and could not relay to you the love you should have been feeling for this Divine Being.

It is never too late to turn your life around and get back on the spiritual pathway by finally accepting that, without God in your life, nothing seems to work! Oh yes, sometimes you feel that life is perfect; you have a good job, a nice home, children to love and cherish... but then one morning you wake up and your whole life has changed! The job you felt was so secure suddenly doesn't exist anymore! Of course you are devastated, and wonder where your life will take you now. The extent of this devastation through the downward spiral your life takes, depends on the *growth your soul needs!* No one knows what another person's karmic lessons are, therefore you can never judge another, or speculate as to why this is happening.

Following a situation such as this, some souls feel a *sense of relief,* because in the very core of their being they sensed that the life they had been leading was not what they really wanted it to be. There was something missing in their lives, but they didn't know exactly what it was. It was only when they finally came face to face with themselves, that they acknowledged that what was missing was a loving personal relationship with God.

The energy on the planet has been changing so drastically, that it is difficult for many of you to continue functioning as you have in the past. The vibrations have been raised so many times over the past ten years that those who have not yet awakened find it hard to understand what is happening around them; they only sense that they don't seem to be in step with universal energy anymore. Each time there is a new wave of energy sent to the planet for her spiritualization, the speeding up of the vibratory rate puts the unawakened **a little more out of step** with everything in their lives. They are not vibrating on the same wave length as others who are aware and understand that they must *go with the flow* in order to keep some semblance of normalcy in their everyday lives.

The *Natural Law of Cause and Effect* – as you sow, so shall you reap – has been affected by the quickening of the vibratory rate or Mother Earth. Because of the density of the energy on the planet, it previously took **up to five years** for the **effects** of *creating your own reality by your way of thinking,* to return to you. With the new energy field around the planet, *your thoughts no longer leave your aura. It is very important to always keep your thoughts positive and loving, as there is a boomerang effect; your thoughts today, will be your reality tomorrow!*

The changes that will take place will be for your highest good. The life experiences which are before you are the ones you had chosen to complete before incarnating in this lifetime. The density of the energy on the planet prohibited you from awakening before. This is part of the karmic plan which was there from the beginning.

The souls awakening now will come to realize that the information they will be given has always been in their subconscious mind, just waiting to come forth when the time was right. We want you to know that it is through no fault of your own that you did not awaken before, as the precise moment of the awakening was chosen before your incarnation.

So many negative things are happening on the planet at this moment. You must be asking where all this violence will lead to and why is God not putting a stop to it. Please know, dear children of Light, that you have always had free will on Planet Earth – the right to make your own mistakes, to learn the lessons you needed for your soul growth.

I, and many other Masters, have been working diligently to prepare for the changes that will take place when Mother Earth takes her final step into the Light and returns to the fifth dimension, from which she originally came.

We are all One, a part of the God Energy which directs everything in the universes. The Creator Father/Mother God has always been in control of what was happening on the planet, although you sometimes questioned this. He/She would only let His *sometimes wayward children* go just so far into the negative energy so that you might learn from your mistakes, then a balance would be brought forth. God would not allow you to destroy the planet, for it is very important for the balance of the whole Universe.

You always had the choice, to learn from your mistakes and move closer to the Light, or self-destruct if you refused to change your attitudes and negative actions. Over the last few years, with the Light having been put so strongly around the planet, many of you have realized that there was no other alternative but to turn to your Creator, to help you reverse the *free fall* you felt you were in.

We realize that much of this might be difficult for you to understand on a mental level, but if you read this with your heart, you will feel yourselves opening more and more to the recollection of who you truly are as the soul. Be true to yourselves and accept who you are, even though you may fear that your family and friends might not understand. Each one is at his or her own level of evolution, and you can never judge the growth of another. You are all mentors for each other, and the lessons can be learned through the positive or negative energy. Some people around you may be the best teachers you have had in this lifetime. Through their negative energy and wrong attitudes, you learned the lesson that *you did not want to be like them;* therefore you worked very hard to be positive and loving, in spite of all that was happening around you. When you realize and accept that everyone in your life has been there for your growth in one way or another, you can bless them for having been a wonderful instrument for the evolution of your soul. You cannot judge another for the role they came to play on the planet in this lifetime. When they return to Spirit, they will be received with open arms for having completed the task and perfectly played their part on *the stage of life.*

Blessed children of the Light, hear me well! Each of you is special in the eyes of God, and is equally loved. No one is better than another, and you are each in the exact place you are supposed to be for the soul growth needed. The problem is that most of you have never learned to love yourselves, and therefore do not have the sense of self worth that you need in order to grow in wisdom and in grace. Believe me when I say that each of you is important in the eyes of the Divine energy, as none of you really know who you truly are as the soul. You may have chosen what you would call a *lowly* life in this incarnation, because there was some aspect of your soul growth over eons that needed **rounding out** – a little lesson that was missed over all your lifetimes which you needed to experience in order to return *Home* as the perfect being you truly are. This is why it is important to hold on to the concept that, when your return to the Spirit World takes place, ***God does not judge you–you judge yourself***. When this happens, you will have the complete remembrance of your soul identity and will realize the reason for every phase of your physical life and the lessons you have learned in this incarnation.

We ask that, through the practice of meditation techniques, you take at least thirty minutes daily to release the stress which so many of you carry in your physical, mental, and emotional bodies. This will connect you with your soul, and create positive, loving energy in your vibration, which will balance the negativity that is created by others around you who have not yet awakened.

Please be aware of the importance of your responsibility to self before your responsibility to others. You have always been taught that you must think of others before thinking of yourselves, which has kept you from learning the important spiritual lesson that your **Beloved Brother Jesus came to the planet two thousand years ago to teach.** He tried very hard to make you understand that to have a balance in your spirituality you must first and foremost love yourselves. When He said : **"Love thy neighbor *as thyself"***, this is exactly what he meant. When you love yourself and feel a sense of self worth you feel in harmony with Spiritual law, in a way that most of you have never known in your lives. On a soul level, you will know who you truly are, and this makes you feel closer to God. You will realize *that it is all right to give to others*, but you will also know *when it is time to receive*, in order to keep a balance in your lives.

Many years hence, when you have attained your complete awakening, you will look back in awe at the person you once were, compared to whom you have finally become. When you realize the growth you have achieved through all those **traumatic experiences**, you will not regret for a moment having experienced them. *You will know in the very core of your being* that they were *necessary* to bring you to the culmination point of who you are as the soul.

The breaking of the dawn of each new day should see you awakening with joy in your hearts, ready to face whatever obstacles will be in your lives that day. Once you accept the fact that *every experience* is for your highest good, you can begin to change your way of perceiving daily life. As each negative happening comes into your vibrational range, it is important that you stay neutral and ask your Higher Self what is the lesson needed. The Higher Self, wanting only the highest good for you, will transfer a thought, often through picture form, into your mind. This will help you to understand why you have attracted the situation into your vibration, and what the needed lesson is. By refusing to let negative energy surface under any circumstances, you neutralize the negativity which for some reason was attracted to you through your *thoughts, words or deeds*.

Be aware of the people around you who are not seeking your highest good. Learn to protect your auric fields from these souls at all times, knowing that negative energy can be as powerful as positive energy. Keep your emotional bodies continually balanced, for the moment you permit negative emotions to surface and throw your vibration out of kilter, your Light is dimmed. It is imperative that you meditate to always reinforce your **Light bodies** which serve as a protective force field that no negative vibrations can penetrate.

We, your Beloved Masters and guides, are close to you to help in any way we can; but you must always remember that you have *free will*, and even we are not permitted to supersede this God given right to all the Earth children. Therefore, in most cases, you must **ask** for our help. Otherwise, we can only stand by and watch because you insist on learning your earthly lessons the hard way. It would be so much easier if only you would look inside yourselves for your answers, which is where they really are. How much pain and suffering could be avoided in your lives!

Always be true to yourselves and do not let others lead you astray from the pathway your soul has chosen. You always know when you are making a wrong choice, or are going against the desires of the soul, as your emotions will surface in a negative way. You must honestly ask yourself if this is what you really want to do, or are you doing it to please or not displease another? Go with your inner feelings, because it is possible that you are being used as an instrument for someone else's growth. Do not let your fears sway you from the decision your soul is helping you to make. You will realize that it turned out for everyone's highest good, whether they understood or not. You are all helping each other in one way or another, and are often used to accelerate another's soul growth.

You are coming into the times when the changes on Earth will overwhelm you. You will start asking questions about the reason for these changes, for there will be occurrences which the earthplane has not previously experienced. Please understand that whatever happens will be for your highest good, and these situations were chosen by you for your soul growth before your present incarnation. As you awaken, more and more will be revealed to you, and the knowledge which is in your subconscious mind will come forth. You will realize that, on an inner level, you have always had this information, but it is only at this moment that you are ready to hear it. Through the soul growth you have received over the past few years, you will recognize it as being ***your truth.***

You will question much of the new information and events in your lives following your awakening. We ask that you seek out someone who has been on the spiritual pathway for a long time to help you understand what is happening; you may also send out a request to your guides for assistance, and they will put someone on your path who will have the answers you need. No request for help to the Spirit World is left unanswered; Spirit will always respond in one way or another, depending on your faith that it shall be so.

Be aware of the atmospheric changes taking place on your planet over the next few years, as Mother Earth prepares to take her final bow as the Being you once knew and originally loved**, *a living Being from which all sustenance flows.*** As mankind descended lower and lower into degradation over the past few centuries, the veneration and love which The North American Indians held in their hearts for Her was forgotten by most of the rest of the Earth population. You forgot to thank Her for everything She gave you with love, because without Her loving generosity you would not have had anything. She suffered greatly from the inhumanity of those She called her children, but Her greatest distress was caused by the realization of what Her beloved children had become, and the depths of decadence into which they had fallen. Be aware dear children, that She loves each of you very much, and wants only the highest blessings for every child of Earth. Her greatest desire is that you awaken and remember the spiritual beings you truly are, and your heritage as a child of God incarnated on the Earth by special permission from your loving Father/Mother/Creator.

    I, Saint-Germain, Master of the Violet Ray responsible for the transmutation of the planet, have a special request to make to each of the beloved children of Earth. I ask that you go forth and take your rightful place in the Universe by being aware of the change in energies around you. I wish you to use the **Violet Ray** to transmute everything in your lives which you are sensing are not for your highest good. By visualizing the Violet Ray above your head, and slowly bringing it down into your whole body through the crown chakra and out through the soles of your feet to be anchored into the earth, you will be transmuting all energies which should not be there. This will bring healing and clearing in many areas of your body. You may also ask for my help in transmuting situations in your lives that you realize must be changed but feel you lack the courage to make such changes on your own. Know that we are always there for you. Please use the Violet Ray to surround others whom you feel need help in transmuting situations in their lives. This powerful Ray will help them to find the courage to make the decisions they know they must make at this point in time. Remember to surround your Beloved Mother Earth with the Violet Ray and also the color pink for the love vibration, which will help her immensely as she prepares to move into her ascension.

Blessings From All of Us!

CHAPTER FIVE

THE HIGHER SELF

ARCHANGEL MICHAEL

Beloved children of the Light, I bring you greetings from the Most High. Know how dearly you are loved! We are aware of the great pressure many of you seeking the Light are experiencing, and of your deep desire to attain the level of spiritual growth to which you aspire.

You must understand that, by being in the physical world, there are things to be accomplished and tasks to be completed before you can move permanently onto your chosen path. You are going through a period of initiation with many tests and trials! In spite of your eagerness to begin on your new pathway, you must discipline yourselves to attend to your worldly duties with willingness and joy. In order to learn the lessons necessary to awaken your ***Higher Self*** and transcend into the new spiritual energy with which you will be working, you must go through many of your experiences on your own. By working through your ***Higher Self***, you will be able to bring your personality and ego under the guidance of your soul, and many spiritual gifts will unfold as your Light is increased.

You are feeling that many experiences in your lives are being played out for the last time and that a new way of life awaits you! You often feel a great sense of joy and exhilaration for which there seems to be no earthly reason. Know that it is so; your soul is finally taking its rightful place in your life and shares the wonder of a new beginning, when it will finally be free to embark on its mission. Even though you don't

consciously understand what is happening, let this beautiful energy permeate your whole being, knowing that something wonderful *is* happening. Accept that a **quantum leap** in your spiritual growth is being taken.

Once you have acquired the growth necessary to access your **Higher Self**, and have brought your ego and personality under the guidance of your soul instead of the other way around, we will be able to assist you through the infusion of greater **Light** into your bodies which will bring wisdom, harmony, and protection from the mass consciousness.

It is time to release the ego, so that your soul may take its rightful place in your lives and bring each of you into your **Mastership**. I want you to know that you are, and always have been **Masters**. Only the density of the earthly energy, and the sleep state into which you fell each time you returned to the planet, kept you from remembering. It was necessary for you to completely forget from where you came, so that you could focus into the energy of the planet in order to work out the karmic patterns and learn the needed lessons.

Try to be aware of our presence around you at different times. In the beginning, you may only sense our energy during your meditation periods or in the sleep state, awakening with a wonderful feeling of being surrounded with love. As you progress in your Spiritual awakening, however, you will sense our presence more often as moments of great joy, which bring you a feeling of happiness unlike anything you have ever known.

When you reach this stage, we can come close enough to help you make many new decisions in your life. You will feel a cold sensation which makes you shiver, and the hair will stand up all over your body. As this begins to happen more and more, it is important that you recognize that we are trying to help you make the right choices in your life–the ones which are for your **highest good** – so that you won't waste time by making mistakes. ***The time for making mistakes is finished!*** Seeing that ***karma*** is terminated on the planet, the lessons you would receive by making these mistakes would be of no use to you, and would only delay the beginning of the important tasks. Time is too precious, and you have much to do!

Know that we have much admiration and love for you for having chosen such hard lessons! Each time you came back to Spirit, the soul remembrance returned, and when you realized that you had not ***gotten your act together*** as you had planned, you wanted to try again. You requested another chance to rectify the mistakes made over and over! Sometimes you wanted to return in a new vehicle almost immediately, possibly within a few earthly years. Other times it would be hundreds of years. But understand that Planet Earth is very unique, as it is the only one in the Universe that has the ***Natural Law of Cause and Effect,*** and is in great demand by those wishing to acquire soul growth. Those given permission by ***The Lords of Karma*** to incarnate here are very privileged!

No matter how strong your desire to complete your ascension, there is still much growth needed in many areas of your lives before this can finally happen! First and foremost, you must have learned to release the density of your physical body, and function only from your Light body.

Many of you have asked for our help in this endeavor. We say to you that you must do your share by joining with others of like mind, which will accelerate the process for your ascension. You may do this on your own, but it will take a longer period of time to come into the full ascension energy needed to completely leave the physical body behind for short periods, and to be able to fully reintegrate that body on your return. We are working with you very closely as this needs to be done over a period of time to make sure that all is balanced. There are many books written to help you understand exactly what is needed in preparation. Once you have the techniques very clearly in your mind, and you feel balanced with them, you must always use the same ones. Each time you become a little stronger, and begin to believe that this is really happening, you will take another step forward in your ascension process.

Be aware of those around you who refuse to believe what is actually happening on the planet. Do not let their negative words or actions deter you from your path. Know that at this moment in time, each soul is where it is supposed to be in its growth. Sometimes they are there to test your faith, but when you **know** in the very core of your being that what is happening with you is **real**, you will no longer allow the skeptics to disturb you. The changes that will be taking place in your lives will be done as gently as possible. With your new vision of what the future entails, you will be able to remain calm, knowing that everything in your life will work itself out as it should. You are exactly where you are meant to be at this moment in time.

As the changes on the planet start taking place, more and more people will be turning towards God for their answers. With your inner depth spiritual awareness, they may realize that possibly you have the answers, and turn to you for information. Go slowly and share with them as much as you think their minds can absorb. Tell them that everything starts by **going within** through daily meditation techniques. Be patient with them, because your mission on the planet at this time may be about helping the newly awakening souls, and you will start by practicing with those around you. It will make it much easier for you to be surrounded by believers, and you may realize that your fear of having to move onto a separate pathway may not be exact. The loved ones around you are really soul mates who are just awakening to their divinity later than you did.

We are aware of the physical problems that so many on the planet face. These are being triggered to come to the surface at this time so that they may realize what they have done to their physical bodies through their negative patterns of thinking. They also must change the food they put into that body, which was meant to be the perfect vehicle for the soul. Detrimental substances such as alcohol and drugs, to which so many earthlings are addicted, must be eliminated. They have their purpose, but are not being used in the way for which they were meant. So many are destroying their lives as well as their families, and it must stop! As we have so often said, the reason for all of mankind's suffering goes back to having moved away from God, leading them into a life of depravation. Much havoc has been reeked on those around them, especially the children, so many of whom no longer can find a stable and loving family life. They need this stability for balance in their lives, in order to become normal, loving human beings when they reach adulthood. Therefore they give what they receive, never having been taught to love themselves and find their proper sense of value. The peer pressure is very strong around them as they reach their teen years. If there has been a breakdown in what should have been a loving family life, they are much more prone to depression and outside influences, which are detrimental to themselves and the growth needed to become responsible loving adults.

We on our side of the veil sometimes cry when we see how lost the little children are, and we try to help them as much as we can. Their need for love is so great that many of them are taking their own lives; they cannot see themselves continuing to live in a world that seems to have no place for them. How can they understand if they were never taught through example to love themselves and others? In their minds, the world is such a bleak place that they cannot fathom continuing to live in what they perceive as being such an inhuman world.

They are not wrong, dear children! Humanity had brought the planet to as low a level as possible without causing it to self-destruct. But we are happy to say that it is finally being reversed, and mankind is on the right pathway through the spiritual awakening that has taken place over the past few years.

This has made it possible for those of us in the World of Spirit to do our part, and put into effect the original plan that has been there since the beginning of the planet. This plan was : that all souls incarnating on Planet Earth would be given free will, and through the **Natural Law of Cause and Effect** would acquire soul growth by returning until they had learned their lessons. You returned over and over with other souls with whom you were working out these lessons, but now it is time to bring down the final curtain on this experiment. Karma is finished on your planet – there is nothing more that can serve you karmic wise through the Law of Cause and Effect. Therefore it is time to bring your beautiful planet back into the fifth dimension from where she originally came eons ago.

Along with the ascension of the planet, so shall all of Mother Earth's beloved children be ascending with Her. She is very excited about this prospect, knowing that She was able to resist all the destruction that has been done to Her and will be returning to take Her rightful place in the Universe. Never for a moment did She stop loving each of you. She understood that you were part of a plan where She was a **schoolhouse** for your soul growth. At times She wondered if you would not go to the limits of your depraved thinking, not realizing that without Her as a living breathing Being, Mankind could not continue to exist. We are thankful that humanity has awakened before it was too late and ***are finally on their way HOME.***

Beloved children, if you could only see the beauty that exists on our side of the veil, which is really only a **thought away.** By changing your perception of what the Heaven World should look like, and opening to letting what it really is, come to you through thought forms and dreams, you would awaken much faster to your Divine heritage. Most of you are already beginning the ascension process in one way or another, especially those souls who have been awakening slowly over a long period of time. For many of you, it started with questions surging to the forefront of your consciousness, and the realization that the earthly churches could not provide answers to which your soul could resonate. At some point you realized that the answers your soul needed were not forthcoming from the **traditional religions,** and you needed to look elsewhere. At that great moment of awakening, you went inside and made your connection with your ***Higher Self,*** turning directly to God and His Heaven World for your answers.

The knowledge which was buried deeply in your subconscious minds and had remained hidden over many lifetimes, began to surface. This was the beginning of the process of the awakening of those in human form–***the Lightworkers* who came to the planet with a mission or important tasks to perform.** Once you awakened, there was no turning back. ***You began to slowly remember who you really were, and what you had come to Earth to do!***

I want you to know that nothing is impossible if **you elevate your consciousness to the spiritual level.** Everything can be created, if what you are requesting is for **your highest good,** or **the highest good of another.** The spiritual gifts of healing, clairvoyance, mediumship, etc. have lain dormant, awaiting the moment when you would release the flow of energy to bring them to their culmination point for you to begin your work. You must put in the effort, dear ones... only you can make the decision to move forward on your spiritual path with an open and loving heart, knowing that this is your destiny. It is time to allow your soul to direct your life in whatever area it wishes to take you, accepting that this was chosen by you before incarnating.

Oh, the wonders that await you, beloved ones! In a short span of your earth time, when you look back to contemplate how far you have come, you will fall to your knees and thank your Father/Mother God for having given you the opportunity of being **Blessed** in this way. But it is we who thank each of you for taking responsibility and answering the **Clarion call** from the Heaven World to awaken and step forth, taking your rightful place in the Universal plan which was prepared eons ago. This could not have been accomplished without the help of all of the loving souls living on the planet. Know that we will be forever grateful to each of you; when you return *Home,* we will be waiting to greet and embrace you. We will hold you in our arms and tell you how special you are for having helped to save Planet Earth and Her inhabitants. We know that Mother Earth will eternally hold a special place for each of you in Her loving heart.

By understanding and having complete remembrance of who you truly are on the soul level, we know that you will release the ego and walk tall. Appreciate how far you have come, and help your earthly brothers and sisters to awaken and take their rightful place in the Divine scheme ***To Restore Heaven On Earth As It Was Originally Meant To Be & The Ascension of Mother Earth Back Into The Fifth Dimension.***

We love you, and I bring Blessings from the Highest.

CHAPTER SIX

AWAKENING SPIRITUALLY

SANANDA

It is a time for new beginnings. Know that you are blessed at this moment in time as we, your beloved guides and Ascended Masters, are waiting for you to open the door and ask for our help and protection in your lives. You are much loved by us all, and we ask nothing more than to take your hand and lead you down the new pathway on which you are about to embark. Awaken and move forward into the new life that awaits each and every one of you. Please know that we are close and can respond instantly to your needs in all areas of your lives.

Eons ago, you had the choice of coming to Earth and living by the law of **free will**, or going to one of the many other planets that exist in the universes. Most of you chose Planet Earth, evolving your soul and learning to work with the **Law of Cause and Effect** – but you had to return over and over, as the lessons your soul needed were not learned.

With the end of **karma** on the planet, many decisions will have to be made as you move forward into the new energy that is permeating the planet to help in your awakening. Do not fear any aspect of the situations you will be facing–sometimes suddenly. You may be taken to the very bottom emotionally but you will emerge from this period of darkness with a great deal of soul growth. These situations will help you to realize that you are not a "kingdom unto yourself"; there are many souls waiting to help you through devastating periods. Everyone goes through moments of depression, and what is lacking is **unwavering faith!** Reach out for the help you need; or if you have gone through your own growth, help others with loving support as they begin to stand tall, finally realizing and accepting who they are as the soul. This is important, my beloved children, as you all must awaken to your true heritage as the Divine soul.

We are aware of the traumas that you are experiencing in your personal lives so that you may take your true places in the LIGHT. Never think that we have abandoned you – we are only a heartbeat away at all times. If you do not feel our presence, it is because *you* have closed the door between our two worlds – it is always open on our side!

The freedom of the soul comes from the final realization that you are not **just a physical body with a mind,** but a being so complex that it is difficult for most of you to understand and accept who you truly are. The day shall come however, when you will each awaken to this realization! You will accept it as the most normal thing in the world and realize that *we are all one.* Only you can keep yourself from understanding and accepting this concept of life in all its dimensions. Be assured that we are doing all we can to help you and are eternally waiting for you to take the first step. The choice must come from you. Hold out your hand as you read this, and say : *"Dear God, I wish to return to the Divine Fold of which I was always a part but have temporarily forgotten my Divine heritage. I ask that I be reunited on a soul level with all my brothers and sisters in the Universe who are assisting me in my awakening. I will allow myself to be who I truly am as the soul and from this day forward I shall only* *permit positive, loving thoughts to enter my mind. SO BE IT!"*

We stand before you with our arms extended, awaiting your call for help. Call on your guardian angels, for they have been with you since you began your many journeys on Planet Earth. They are there for your protection, and will bring you the comfort you need during some of the lowest moments in your lives. Ask for their help with many of the personal problems with which you wrestle in day to day living. Sometimes they will help you out of a dangerous situation. They may even save your physical life if it is not your time to return to the Spirit World. More and more humans are sharing their experiences with their guardian angels, for often this is the moment of their *true awakening.* Through their courage in sharing these personal experiences – some of which may have occurred twenty or thirty earth years ago – millions will be awakened. Others will realize that the experiences they have kept hidden for so long for fear of being ridiculed, were also happening everywhere on the planet. They no longer have to hide their feelings, and can finally accept who they are. For some, it will make them question why their lives were saved at that moment, and what they really came to Earth to accomplish. A new door will open in their awareness and there will be no turning back. They will never be the same again! As this happens, many changes will take place in their lives, as a new destiny path begins to unfold. **Like attracts like;** as they open to their own spiritual awareness, they will draw to them evolved souls on the planet who have been accelerating their spiritual growth over many years. Their task in this incarnation is to help the **newly awakening souls** progress towards the LIGHT.

During my incarnation as *Jesus, the Christ*, I tried to make humanity understand the teachings I had come to bring.

Most were not understood, and were taken even more out of context over the two thousand years since.

At that point in the history of the Earth, there was a great need for a giant leap in consciousness. I was the one chosen to bring this to you. I regretted that you did not understand what was happening at that time, or the message I had come to bring to you. But *know*, dear children, that you only awaken when you are ready, through attaining the soul growth necessary for this to happen. Many more lessons were needed on the planet for the awakening, **and the time is now**!

New doors will be opening for you as you take your first step towards your spiritual awakening. Fear must be put aside as you approach each new event in your lives with joy, anticipating wonderful experiences. First and foremost, you need the faith to understand that whatever happens will be for your highest good and greatest soul growth. As something happens in your life, no matter how different it may seem, you must have perfect faith. Remember : *God is in His Heavens and all is well!* You must **know in the very core of your being**, that something wonderful will come out of this experience, if you will only ***TRUST***.

Be careful of those who will try to prevent you from evolving spiritually. They refuse to listen to the murmurings of their soul. Instead, they continue to listen only to their ego, which refuses to relinquish control. Bless them and let them go their way. They will have their own awakening experience another time, but you must not let yourselves be deterred from your soul path. Each of you is a Divine being in your own right, and some are much more evolved than others. You are often instruments for each others growth. It is through trials and tribulations that the soul *comes into its own, and remembers*

who it truly is. We ask that you learn to love each other unconditionally and let each awaken at his or her own pace. Due to the acceleration of the vibrations on the planet, the ***boomerang effect*** of the Sowing and Reaping will provide them with the lessons they need.

Be aware of the spiritually advanced children around you who have come to the planet to play their part in the ascension plan. Look into their eyes and connect with their souls, that you may help them remember as quickly as possible what they came to the planet to do, in what may be their last lifetime on the Earth Plane. Many of them do remember who they are, and they must grow up quickly to be ready to complete their mission. If you do not **close them down by ridiculing them or refusing to believe the wonderful things they tell you,** you will find children as young as three or four Earth years, with astounding wisdom. They will speak of their lives in Spirit before coming to Earth, and talk of the angels who guard and keep them. Many of them have great powers of healing, which they brought with them in this lifetime as part of their mission.

We are forever grateful to all the children of Light who have awakened and are taking their responsibilities as the Divine beings they truly are. We understand that it is not easy to awaken from what seems a long period of darkness. Be assured that many Light Beings from our side are waiting to help you in every area of your lives. The knowledge, with which you have been indoctrinated on Planet Earth for hundreds of years, cannot leave your conscious and subconscious minds overnight. The density of the energy on the planet and in your bodies kept you from realizing the truth. You were still in the karmic patterns which you had been working out since the beginning of the planet. Some of you had agreed to come when Earth began, as the first and only planet in the universe to have *free will*. Many of you have had thousands of incarnations on this planet, so don't wonder why you are so physically attached to it. Each lifetime was a learning experience to help you perfect your soul.

At some point in the evolution of Mother Earth, your twelve DNA strands were reduced to two. This was through the intervention of beings from another planet, who did not desire the Earthlings to progress as was the original plan, and were looking for control. Your DNA strands are your genetic codes, unique in each human being. Rarely can the same code be found in two different people, unless they are identical twins – two halves of the same sperm egg.

With the spiritualization of the planet, and the help of advanced souls who have been given the techniques from the Spirit World, the ten missing strands can now be reconnected. This will help you evolve more quickly in your spiritual growth, as the memories of who you truly are come to the surface of your being.

As you become more and more aware of the beginning of your new life on Earth, each of you shall be given everything that you need to advance on your pathway. Many changes will occur as the cleansing and clearing takes place in all of your bodies. They may seem unbelievable, but are necessary for the new energies with which you will be working, and from which you will be functioning. As your physical bodies release the density which it has known for eons, the strange sensations which you will be feeling may make you fearful at times. At these moments you must put your complete faith in your beloved guides, who are always there for you.

As you continue to evolve on your spiritual pathway at a much faster pace, the world as you always knew it may seem completely alien to you. There will be times when you will question your sanity. You will sometimes feel out of focus with everyone around you, and wonder if you are becoming mentally and emotionally unbalanced. Many *flashbacks* of experiences in this lifetime will occur, especially those from your childhood years. They were buried deeply, because your soul considered them too traumatic for you to remember on a conscious level. These blockages have hindered your growth, and will be surfacing to be cleared and released. Every negative experience, that has stayed in your subconscious mind from all of your lifetimes, must be released so that you may learn to detach on an emotional and physical level. Through this clearing, the emotional body can finally be balanced and vibrate only to the energy of love.

With the ending of karma on Planet Earth, there is no longer the potential for soul growth through the mistakes you make. **The Law of Cause and Effect**, which was part of the Natural Law for the spiritual advancement of the Earthly beings in each incarnation, no longer holds true. The mistakes you make from continuing to listen to the ego, rather than your Higher Selves, only serves to hinder your progress on your spiritual pathway.

As you evolve spiritually, understanding in greater depth the changes taking place in the energy field of the planet and learning to *flow* with the energy in and around you, ***you will come to realize that you are the Master of your destiny!*** When you learn to function from a complete sense of inner peace at all times, you will be in control of every moment of your life. You will attract to your vibration only the people and experiences which are peaceful. Very gently, one at a time, the unawakened souls will move away from your auric field or if it is their time to do so they will be transformed by the spiritual energy they sense flowing from you.

The awakened ones who have truly found their pathway of **self-realization** are *transmuters* for everyone and everything around them. Often they do not realize it is happening, but their spiritual energy is being *tapped* and used for transmutation in many areas. It can trigger the energy to bring others into alignment with their Higher Selves, if this is their desire – or release physical, mental, and emotional problems.

Millions of souls are truly awakening to their Divinity all over the planet. We want you to be aware of those newly awakening souls at every moment, so that you may consciously, or unconsciously, project the energy needed for their transmutation. This can happen wherever you may be. The circumstances may be serious or comical, because some need the energy of laughter to help them take that final step into their awakening. Remember that the soul loves growth acquired through laughter. It can even happen more quickly, because the energy field of the person has already been lightened by the feeling of joy. They may be laughing at themselves as they remember that all the things they scoffed at for so long, are possibly true. These souls, however, are the best ones to awaken. They are already on their way and will advance very quickly, because they can laugh at themselves and close the door immediately to their old way of thinking. Others are also attracted, believing that there really must be something to this new energy and spirituality they have been hearing about for so long, but had always refused to accept.

We want you to step forward and make a commitment with an open mind and heart, realizing that there is a whole new world opening up to you, and the choice you have made is the right one. The greater the effort you put into letting go of the material and physical world, the faster you will move forward into the Light. Each new day that dawns will bring a greater sense of inner peace, as you realize that things are falling into place in your lives. Everything becomes more effortless as you learn to listen to your Higher Self and make the decisions it is influencing you to make.

As you move forth with greater faith, all doors will open to you. Plans for your new life pattern will seem so simple that you will wonder why you didn't think of them before; but **know,** dear child of Light, that you only awaken when the time is right. Let there be no sense of guilt that you **should have done this years ago**. Now that you know the truth you can move forward at a much faster pac, and help others in their awakening. Even though you may think you are only beginning your own evolution, the truth is that you are *a very old soul!* You came to the planet to awaken at this point in time, to help trigger the remembrance in others of who they are, as the soul energy begins to gently seep into their conscious mind.

With the acceleration of the energy on the planet, which permits you to go directly to the source through your soul for your answers, you no longer waste time. You **know and accept** that what your soul is directing you to do will be for your highest good and greatest growth.

As you advance on your pathway your vibrations will become so light that you will sometimes feel as if you could fly. At these moments more and more joy enters your heart until it feels overflowing. Be aware of these moments of joy, for each time it happens will be a giant step forward in your ascension process. Take the hand of those around you, and let them sense the joy vibrating in your heart. Let this energy surround them. They will want to understand more and be in your presence frequently to sense the love that flows from you at these moments. Be aware of the little children, and include them in this energy. They will take a giant step forward in their growth and awakening. You will be surprised at how quickly they will mature, as they know on a soul level that they have not much time to prepare themselves for their mission. Many will start at a very young age – only a few years in Earth time. Their growth will advance by leaps and bounds as they are included in your energy exercises for your own ascension.

As you move forward on your new path all the souls who are to be a part of the blessed work you will be undertaking, will move onto your pathway one by one. These beings were with you in the Spirit World and in many other Earthly incarnations. With each one you meet there will be a very strong soul connection and an inner sensing that you have always known this person. You will realize that you will be working together in the final phase of your chosen task, helping to awaken Humanity to its Divinity, and the Ascension of Mother Earth.

My beloved children, because of the acceleration of the vibrations and the changes which are about to take place on the planet, I must speak very clearly to you. To those who have not already taken their rightful place in the Divine plan which the Creator prepared eons ago, I cannot express how important it is that your work begin immediately! As we have said before, Planet Earth is very important to the Heavenly Father/Mother God, as well as to the inhabitants of the other planets. Earth was always known as the **JEWEL** because of Her beauty when viewed from outer space. Much damage has been done to Her, but with the help of an ***awakening humanity,*** this will be reversed. She shall once again take Her rightful place in the Universe as the most beautiful planet that exists. She suffered greatly from the inhuman treatment and indignities that were bestowed upon Her, by those whom She considered Her ***beloved children,*** but She always forgave as She did her best to continue to nourish you in every way She possibly could. Now it is your turn to surround Her with love and healing energy, as She goes through the throes of Her own healing. It is imperative that you help Her regenerate, by replanting the trees you have destroyed, and cleaning Her air and oceans, which have been polluted to the point of nearly destroying your race. I don't think you realize how close you came to self destruction!

We are pleased to tell you that, following a few years of cleansing and balancing, Mother Earth will be *whole* once again. We do not say that these times will be easy, but each of you will be exactly where you are supposed to be. Those who chose, before incarnating, to not go through these difficult times, will return to spirit soon; but know that this was their choice – they made this decision as the soul.

I wish to leave you this day with a message of love and hope! Know that you are dearly loved and much admired by all in the Spirit World, for being on Mother Earth at this most important time in the history of humanity. Always remember that this was a choice you made as the soul. Along with the glory of having had the privilege of being on Planet Earth when She prepared to make Her Ascension, goes the shake ups in every area, as She brings herself back into balance. Know that we are close, and you may call on us at all times. Even though the ride may be a little rough, we want you to enjoy the trip on your return to your original Home with us in the Spirit World.

Once Mother Earth is cleared, cleansed, and back to Her beautiful self once again, you may choose to return for another incarnation – but this time it will be different. Planet Earth will be inhabited by loving beings who have finally learned all of their lessons.

Blessings from us all!

CHAPTER SEVEN

LOVE AND COMPASSION

MOTHER MARY

The time is drawing nigh, dear children, when many changes shall take place in your lives and on your beautiful Planet Earth.

I have come many times to warn you about conditions that would be occurring, but now I want to say that the alterations will not be as drastic as they would have been had you not turned your lives around and moved back into the Light through the understanding of who you are as the soul.

As they awaken to their Divinity, many beings on the planet are finally beginning to believe. It has taken much devastation and sorrow for this to happen; but now is the time to reverse the negativity and move forward into the Light, becoming the enlightened beings you originally were, and to which you will soon be returning.

We are aware of the worries concerning the catastrophic events which have been prophesied over hundreds of years; but I want you to understand that the Earth children are awakening, taking their destiny in hand, and reversing these predictions of destruction. Many of these lessons are no longer needed and, due to these changes, a bright future for Mother Earth and her children is much more assured. You may dispel the fears; we want you to know that you will be safe. As you grow in wisdom and understanding, listening to the **inner voice**, your

Higher Self will guide you as to where you should be when the clearing and cleansing on the planet really begins.

You know, dear ones, through your ignorance and lack of understanding, you have done great harm to Mother Earth! You have forgotten that She is a living Being from which all sustenance comes, and without whom Mankind cannot survive. Now She must do the necessary work to heal Herself. Most of you will be on the planet during this time; but as we said, the destruction would have been greater had Humanity not awakened.

We deeply care about each of you; your beloved guides and angels are close to you. In each lifetime The Father/Mother God sends an angel as a guiding force into whose care you are given, and these angels have been with you since your first incarnation on Planet Earth.

For eons, you didn't remember that you had this **Special Being**... this perfect helper who can instantly be at your side the moment there is danger or you need help in some capacity of your life. Without your even being aware of them, they prevented many drastic situations from happening. Sometimes they protected your life during an accident, or a grave illness to your physical body because you broke all the natural, spiritual and karmic laws of the Universe, and brought yourself to death's door. In desperate moments you called out for Divine help, and they were immediately by your side. When you remembered these dramatic moments, you often said : "It was a miracle!", even though many times you did not remember *sensing the presence or seeing this Special Being,* in whose care you had been placed by the Spirit World since your Earthly birth.

It was necessary for you to go through many lessons before you finally began to understand that some of the things you had been taught as children through your Bible and Spiritual teachings were true. They were often misunderstood however, as they were not always taught correctly. Now, through the awakening of your own soul, this precious knowledge is coming to the forefront, and you are able to receive your own answers from your Higher Self. It is important that you listen to your soul at every moment, so that you may always make the right decisions. Much work must be done to your ego, which needs to be released in order to hear the *still small voice* coming from the depths of your soul, telling you what to do and where to be. It gives you the answers to your questions through the feeling center, helping you to realize when you are making a mistake, by having an *inner feeling* **that all is not well... something is wrong, take a second look at this situation!**

I have been close to the Planet since my incarnation two thousand years ago, as the ***Mother of the Christed Being.*** I was blessed to have been chosen as the vehicle to bring this ***Beloved Master*** to the Planet at a time when ***Spiritual Knowledge was so greatly needed.*** Many did not understand the ***True Teachings of the Natural, Spiritual and Karmic Laws*** that ***Jesus*** brought to the Earth plane; but now you are realizing the truth as it was given at that point in time.

We want you to know that we are very close, and will help in any way we can. You need to go back to praying, as this helps you to keep focused and balanced... connected with the God energy. The energy of prayers floating up towards the Ethers and Heaven World is very powerful and precious in the eyes of God, and is instantly received. You must follow your request by keeping your heart and mind open **so that you may** hear and recognize the answer when you receive it. He always answers your prayers in one way or another! You must also have the *faith* that the answer you receive will be the *right* one, although you may not believe it at the time. Only later will you understand that it was the one needed for your *highest good*, and you will realize why it had to be so.

You are never alone as you sense The Father/Mother God's presence around you. He sends his workers to be close to you and help you, to sustain you through moments of despair as loved ones are returning to our side. But do not mourn them, dear children; they are only returning Home, from where they originally came. As the *soul,* they have chosen to do so at this point in time. They have finished the tasks they chose to do, and the lessons they needed to learn on the planet. Sometimes it is through a loved one returning to Spirit that those around them receive the greatest *soul growth!* Often it is through regrets : "If only I had done this or said that, given them more love, etc.", but *know* that nothing can be changed... that it is too late. That is why you must do it now! Every moment of your day, keep your vibration positive and your attitude loving, understanding that there is a dire need for love on the planet. It is important that you let this love flow from your heart chakra to all the souls around you – in the family, your work area, all over the planet, where there is much devastation taking place.

There will be changes in many areas of your lives. Receive these with joy, knowing that they are for your soul growth. On some level you requested them because you were ready to open to the Light that is flowing in from the Universe, to help make the changes that are coming for the *Ascension of Planet Earth.* We have spoken of this for many years, but unfortunately few have listened. As the changes take place, you will know more and more what your role is to be for this wonderful *Event* which has been prophesied since the beginning of time, but was not understood.

Mother Earth can no longer function in the destructive atmosphere that has been around Her for eons, and which was worsening; but now She is very happy to feel the change in the energy field which surrounds Her, and She is doing Her clearing and cleansing, bringing the Light back into Her body.

You will realize more and more that you will be receiving help from other planets, even though you didn't want to believe or accept that there was life on the millions of planets in the Universes. There always has been life, and some of them often came very close to you. As the changes begin, they will be approaching you more and more to make their presence known, and to help those they consider *Earthlings.* They want to let you know that they come as brothers and sisters in love and understanding, and they want to be your neighbors. Open to them, but make sure that you protect yourselves until you can learn to vibrate to their energy. There are many species of Beings on different planets who do not resemble Earthly Beings, but their physical differences should not make you believe they are not normal. They want to know you and be able to better understand your planet, as we are sure you would like to know more about theirs. They often come close to study the Earth species, for your ways of life have intrigued them for eons.

I have come to bring you a message of love, harmony and awareness through the surfacing of the **knowledge of who you are as the soul**, and **the understanding of the importance of being true to yourselves.** Do not let others make your decisions for you! Be aware of those on your pathway who want to keep you from knowing who you truly are *in the very*

core of your being. You have a Divine pathway to follow, and the pathway of others is not for you. By listening to your **Higher Self** – *the still small voice within* – you will know where your lifepath is taking you, and where you are destined to be.

We are close and try to help through the love vibration that we bring to you. Often you sense our presence. We surround you with our loving energy to let you know that you are Divine, that you are special and much loved.

This feeling seems to be coming from somewhere that is not of yourself. When you have periods of highs and lows, when you are going through difficult times and you feel as if your world is not always treating you right, as you sense yourself enveloped in what feels like a **warm blanket of love,** you question where this wonderful feeling comes from.

It is important that you have your ***down*** periods until you learn to recognize that it is during these moments of depression in your lives that your light is dimmed. When your light is bright, it is projecting out all over the world, enveloping others of like mind who also need your help.

During your meditations, it is important that you send out this Light to surround all of the Earth children. They are going through very difficult times as they awaken to their Divinity, especially those who do not believe in a Spiritual life and have no inkling that anything else exists besides their physical bodies and their minds. They do not want to understand anything different, but they will be turned around quickly as the changes start taking place on the Planet.

Love and Compassion

They will look for a refuge, a spot where they can feel safe, but they will not find it. They must look inside themselves to find the answer. They will be led in the proper direction, but they must find their answers *inside* themselves, rather that *outside,* where they have always searched for them.

It is sad to see so many young people destroying their lives through the use of drugs and alcohol. These devastating situations are bringing many of them back to us before their time! They need to understand that they are important in the eyes of God, and they have their place in the Universe. This incarnation was very important for them to grow and awaken Spiritually. They will begin to feel that there is something wrong in their lives, as though an anchor were missing! They have alienated everyone around them, and feel they have no one to whom they can turn for help. As they feel their weaknesses, they no longer trust themselves, and begin to wonder if it is too late to reverse the damage they have done. They realize they are destroying their lives, as well as their physical bodies. When this happens, they will awaken if they are ready to do so. Otherwise they will be taken care of by the loving Beings on our side.

The soul cannot be destroyed, but is sad that it cannot help the vehicle in which it dwells to perform the tasks for which it incarnated. Because of destructive patterns learned early in life through negative attitudes, the ego chose to retain control of the mind and physical body, and will possibly destroy them in one way or another. Sometimes the Soul will cut the silver cord and return to Spirit, as it refuses to abide in a physical body which is of no use to it. Many times, in what is considered an accident, this is what occurs – the Soul simply decided to **return *Home!***

Other souls chose to come to the planet and live these experiences to be an example of what these terrible plagues can do to the human mind and body, and to the lives of the loved ones around them. Many families had to learn to deal with the destructive paths on which their loved ones had embarked. But through the interaction of the karmic lessons being worked out in these situations, there was a possibility for much soul growth.

We want you to know, dear children, that you are very Blessed! We want you to know that you are loved, and that we are close to you. Although you must ask for our help because you still have **Free Will,** many times we help you without your even knowing we are there. If we see a situation in which we need to intervene, especially if we feel there is a danger that the soul will be released from the physical body before its time, either through a grave illness or an accident... we may come to your aid if this is under Divine ordinance. Many times, this is what is known on your planet as a ***Near Death Experience.*** It is not the time for the soul to end its ***Earthly Sojourn!***

I ask that you help the little ones... those Blessed little Beings that are enduring so much abuse on your Planet. They are **so innocent**, and are not responsible for what is happening to them! They have been given to you by God The Father to love and cherish, but instead millions of little ones are being destroyed – physically, mentally and emotionally! ***You need to return to love!*** But *first* you must learn to love yourselves! We are aware of the devastating situations surrounding the human beings at this point in time, but know that all will be balanced; many of these detrimental situations will awaken humanity to their Divinity. As others hear about the terrible occurrences the children are experiencing, they realize how important their little ones are to them. But they need to do more, even if it is only giving them more love. Help them to awaken to their Divinity. The only reason it was lost along the way is because it was forgotten when they came into the physical body. Many of them were not taught to love God, or even that God existed! They need examples to follow. As the parents and family members of these beloved little ones, you are responsible for seeing that they are taken care of, loved and nurtured. In turn, they may grow to become loving adults, closely connected to their souls, the Divine side of themselves, realizing and remembering who they truly are. Tell them that you love them and that God loves them. Tell them that Mary, their Mother in Heaven loves them. Tell them to pray to me and ask for my help and Blessing, and I will be there for them. When they are very young, teach them to kneel in prayer and to go inside themselves. This has been lost on the planet, as your Governments decided prayer was no longer to be permitted in the schools. Some of them would like to pray, but because their siblings and friends do not wish to do so, they are afraid of being different. Tell them it is all right to love God and themselves, and to ask for the Divine help that they need. Whether it is in a school situation – an exam they are writing, etc., whatever their needs are – if they keep their connection to the Spiritual part of themselves, they will have their answers and be protected.

Sick individuals are kidnapping the children! All over the Planet, God's little ones are disappearing. The human minds, both male and female, are becoming twisted and depraved, and these little children cannot protect themselves. These sick minds are connected to the negative side of the Spirit World. Do know that there are many negative entities close to you at this point in time, and you are all very vulnerable to this energy. You have forgotten how to protect yourselves through prayer, calling on the **Light**, and by allowing your own Spiritual knowledge to come to the forefront of your Being.

It is important that you meditate, and that you teach the little ones to meditate. This should be taught in all of your schools; each morning should start with a prayer and a few moments of meditation. However, we understand that you have *free will;* and because of the many different religions amongst you, there are those who do not wish one belief system to be more prevalent than another.

Within two years you will see many changes. People will be turning back to God, asking for help, searching in their hearts and souls for reasons why things are happening on the planet. They will have no choice, as they will have nowhere else to turn when Mother Earth starts shaking as she goes through her cleansing. Know that you will be protected; that you will always be in the right place at every moment *if* you stay connected with your *inner self* and are able to hear your answers and any warnings we might be giving you concerning your safety.

It is very important for you to be **grounded!** You must learn to function with the new energy that currently exists, staying connected to your *Higher Self* as well as your Earthly connection. The decisions you make must be the right ones at every moment.

As you draw closer to the *Ascension*, there will be few new souls coming into the Planet, as they will not have time to grow to adulthood. You will notice that fewer babies will be born. Also, as humanity begins to realize that they cannot feed the children they already have, changes in thinking will take place. They will *choose* to only have the number of children they can afford to feed and have time to love and nurture.

Love and Compassion

A child is a gift from God, to be loved and nurtured until the time when they return *Home* to our side. We understand that, when many of you were growing up, you did not receive the love, understanding and Spiritual knowledge needed to help you to grow in wisdom and in faith. However, as the new energy of the Love vibration surrounding the Planet enfolds you, you will feel an inner awakening taking place. **It will be as if someone were knocking at the door of your heart and requesting entrance**. Your *Beloved Jesus* always promised that he would be there for you. He said : *"I stand at the door of your heart and knock, and you only have to invite Me to enter, and I will abide there."* From this moment on your heart **will be filled with Love and glowing Light.** This Light will flow out to those around you, and all over the Planet till the end of eternity. It is very important, dear children, that you request His presence to help you and the little ones... He is very close to each of you. Even though Jesus understands the karma working out on the Planet, He is very sad to see what is happening to the little ones. Be aware of their plight and give them love.

Once you have the Love and Light in your heart, let it flow out of your house and into the houses of your neighbors. If you could only realize the changes which could occur by doing this! Because of the negativity and the horrible things happening, we understand that you are living in fear of everything and everyone around you; but the changes must begin in the heart! By letting the love flow out to your family, helping them to become loving beings, they may also open their hearts and let the love flow.

You do not have to be close to someone to do this. You may sit in a chair in your home and let the love flow from your heart, visualizing pink Light going to the houses in your neighborhood, enveloping each one. Keep all the houses around you enveloped in this pink Light, and realize how their occupants are changing. You will be surprised at how loving thoughts from you can alter their lives!

Always having a smile for everyone helps a great deal to release the fear in others, because they realize that your lack of fear means you have something special**... a space in which a part of you abides, which keeps you from being fearful.** As you protect yourself and your family, keeping everyone in the Light, ask that the children be protected by their guardian angels as they leave for school in the morning.

Start immediately to project Light around your schools, that the children who are not loved elsewhere may at least receive a little love and understanding there. From your heart to their heart, as you focus your Light on the schools which your children attend, surround the building with love. Try to be involved in what is happening in that school as much as you can, at least with the meetings with other parents, so that you may bring your Light to these sessions. Help them understand that arguments are not the only ways to be productive. Take a certain degree of responsibility for the homes on each side of you by your loving thoughts. Do not judge... just surround them with Light and put them in your prayers! Through your energy field, you may call on the Divine Beings to stay close to them. It is important that you realize that your prayers are answered in one way or another. The powerful love of the Father/Mother God surrounds everyone, and **miracles do happen.** They are at your fingertips; they only need the right energy to produce them. You can do this, dear ones. You have the power to create miracles every moment of the day. Each time that you succeed, **your power becomes stronger.** Others will realize that something is happening, and will want to know what you are

Love and Compassion ~105

doing. Start practicing on little things, and thank God for everything that happens in your life – no matter how unimportant it may seem! This will attract more positive action and help from the Other Side, and greater miracles will begin to occur.

At times, situations take place which don't seem fair from your understanding of life and love. Realize there is karma working out in every situation. Some souls incarnated to sacrifice themselves, so that mankind may realize how low they have fallen.

No matter what is happening on the Planet, know that you will be safe. Know that many souls will be returning to Our Side because they chose to do so before incarnating. Some of them chose to be victims, to be an example of how depraved mankind has become! Some of these souls are part of the destruction and killings taking place all over the planet, often in **The name of God.** As they fight over their religions, it is the children who are the most vulnerable in these situations. Know that these little souls, unbeknown to their human consciousness, chose this seemingly untimely death on an unconscious level. The tragic circumstances of their early demise would awaken souls all over the planet, encouraging others to take responsibility on a personal and global level. When these little ones return to Spirit, we will be waiting for them. Someone had to serve as the instruments for mankind to realize what is really happening out there!

The world as you know it is changing. As you see the examples of all the negative happenings on the planet, you will know that there is Divine Order; these examples are being given for your awakening so that, on a deeper level, you may realize what is happening.

Many illnesses as you now know them will be disappearing from the Planet. As humanity awakens, they will understand that they can heal themselves by looking towards alternative medicines. Although they have always been there, you are only now beginning to discover them and put them to use to help mankind. There is a cure for every illness which exists on your planet in plants and herbs. You are beginning to find them, and are realizing what miracle medicines they are. They are part of God's Earthly Plant Kingdom and will heal, not harm, your physical body. They start by healing the attitudes... and as the attitudes change, the body heals itself. Your body cannot stand negativity over a long period of time without breaking down; something has to give somewhere. Except for some cases where karma is involved, ***all illness is self inflicted*** through the Natural Law of **Cause and Effect**. Sometimes the illness was chosen in a manner so that the family members, friends, and loved ones around them would grow from having gone through the experience of losing a loved one.

It is always devastating to lose a child whom you dearly loved, but even though it may be difficult for you to understand, accept that it was a choice that the soul made. At some point you will understand why this had to happen, although it may only be when you meet again on the **Other Side.** You could meet with them during the sleep state, as you open the door to other states of consciousness during your dreams, or they could visit you any time in your home in their Astral body, if you accept that **they are not dead**. They will sense that you are open to their presence and will joyfully welcome their visit. They are more **alive** than you are, as their Spirit body lives on, and they can come to you anytime they wish through instant thought.

If you are open to this concept, you will **sense their presence each time they enter your home. You can talk to them and love them... and let them love you.** They will come close to you and try to help you. Sometimes they are devastated when you do not sense their presence, especially the little ones who have passed very quickly, sometimes in ways that left them very traumatized. It is important that you keep them in your thoughts, projecting love and light to help them as they move forward into the Light. Help them to release the trauma they went through as they left the physical body. The shock of their passing stays temporarily, but know that there are spirits there to help them when they do pass over. They take care of them until they awaken to who they really are as the soul, recalling their other lifetimes, and remembering what they had come to do in this incarnation. They will realize whether or not they completed the karma they had chosen. Let them help you, as they wish to do so and are close to you, but you must also release them by accepting their decision to return to the Heaven World. Give them unconditional love that they may continue to advance on their pathway in the Spiritual realms, because *there is no death,* dear children. It is important that you understand and accept this at every moment.

I wish you to know that I am close to you, and await your request for help. Send up your prayers and needs into the Ethers, and someone will receive them. The Spirit World is only a thought away, and you must send up that thought with love, asking for our help and we will be there for you. You may pray for another human being, those prayers will be heard also, and we will help them if your request is made with love.

I want you to know that my love flows to you always and forever. I will be there for you at anytime you need my help, to comfort and to bring the love that you need as you learn to unconditionally love yourselves. You must work on that, dear ones; this is the answer to all of your problems. Everything will work out in your life once you yourself are in balance. Your loved ones will come into balance also, or they will move off your pathway. You must love them unconditionally, and let them be who they are; but you must first start by learning to love yourselves unconditionally. The rest will grow and evolve from there. As those around you realize that you have changed, they will want to know what is happening... why you are serene and happy in spite of the conflicts going on around you. This is where you must refuse to take responsibility for everybody else's happiness! You owe them unconditional love; try to help them to understand. Counsel them with love and talk to them of God; but if they refuse, it is their Divine right to do so. You must not take responsibility for their mistakes, which are their learning lessons. They have choices to make from the time they are very small, and they grow from learning through these experiences. When they get tired of attracting negative experiences to their lives, if they see you smiling and serene in spite of what is going on in the world around you, the love that flows from your heart will help them to change. If not, they may move off your pathway because they cannot stand the density of your **Light,** which disturbs their negativity.

Sometimes you cannot help your own family members. This is when you must learn to **release, let go and let God**, because He is there every moment. When you cannot help them, it is because they have something to learn on their own. You must step back, Bless them, and surround them with Light. Be there for them if they need to talk; when they start to awaken, you can gently step back into the picture, but do not take responsibility for them. They are responsible for themselves, and will grow at their own rhythm and in their own time. Just keep them in your prayers, and ask God to protect them.

I love you, Dear ones... keep me in your heart. Ask me to protect you and your loved ones, and I will do so. Remember, you still have free will.

I am Mother Mary

I give you my Blessing, and I bring you the Blessing of the Father/Mother God, Creator of The All That Is, and of My Beloved Son whom you knew as Jesus the Christ.

CHAPTER EIGHT

AN AWAKENING HUMANITY

ST.-GERMAIN

This is a year of many changes on Planet Earth; shake ups in every domain with many new doors opening for the beloved children. Many do not understand exactly what is happening, but they know that there are changes taking place inside themselves and in their lives, as well as all over the Earth Plane. Some are fearful, but they are mostly those who still see themselves as a **physical body,** and put much importance on the physical side of life. Replace sadness with joy, perfect understanding, and acceptance of the changes in your lives, as you awaken to who you truly are as the soul. There will be new paths for each of you; you will wonder which way you are to go. Listen to the ***still small voice in your heart,*** and you will know immediately which is the right path for you. We are all very close and are helping with the transition period on the planet, especially working with the Violet Ray to help with the transmutation of all the negative energy around the Earth at this point in time.

We want you to sow love in your lives and let it spread to everyone around you, that it may go forth all over the planet and awaken others to their divinity. We understand that there is much negativity on Mother Earth, but do not fear, all is under Divine Order. There is a purpose for everything that happens.

Each of you has a destiny path which is under Divine Guidance and you know what your pathway is, even if presently it is only on a subconscious level. As you allow the spiritual energy to enter your lives on a daily basis, everything will open to you. The new pathway on which you will be embarking will be easy to recognize, as you will have an inner feeling that somehow you have always known this. It is only then that you will understand its purpose.

You chose to be there to embark on the pathway which will lead to your enlightenment as well as the enlightenment of other souls on the planet. You have much work to do, and we ask that you step out with courage and fortitude, knowing that what you do will be the right things for you and everyone else who is put on your pathway to receive your help. Many of you are teachers and healers. Each of you has a destiny path, and you must look inside yourselves for the answers, because that is where they are.

As you awaken each day, we ask that you connect with the energy of the Universe and flow with this wonderful energy the whole day through. Tune into the Godhead energy, asking each day that you be put in the right place to help many other souls awaken to their divinity. They must be given the necessary information to help them understand what is happening in their lives as well as on the planet.

It is very important that this information be shared with all the Earth children who are ready to understand. We are close to you, to help you undertake the changes that are happening in your lives. Also that you may realize the importance of getting this information to those in need of understanding this work. We are not separate from you; we are close to you at all times. You only have to say our names, and we are with you. Be it only in thought, it is as close as if we were there in the physical body, standing right beside you.

There are many things about our dimension that you do not understand. This information shall be given to you very soon because the Spiritual teachings must be brought forth and given to the Earth children. They must go forward on their pathway knowing that every moment is precious and should not be wasted. Each moment should be used for something positive rather than negative; for growth rather than destruction; for love rather than violence. Understand that changes are taking place on your planet, and in a short period of time many countries in distant places will start their awakening also.

The violence that is there will not always be so. We are working with all the countries to change their consciousness, to bring the Light into their thought process, that they may see **Light** rather than darkness, as they presently do. This will change their way of thinking even though they don't understand why. The awakening shall take place in every country in the world. Mankind will begin standing up for themselves, letting everyone *know* who they are, and the changes that must be made in every facet of their lives for the highest good of all. It is important that all men and women stand together facing the conflicts and the destruction that is there on the planet.

We ask that each of you who has awakened do your share in bringing this information forth so that peace might reign all over the Earth. You may also help by keeping the countries that are in conflict in your prayers, and surrounding the planet with the violet light for transmutation during your periods of meditation. We are working with them, but the information that they are divine beings and must awaken to their divinity, should come from other countries. They will begin to know you as brothers and sisters in light and love. In turn they will extend a hand to help other countries that are closer to theirs with their awakening process.

All humanity must understand that they are God's precious children; **they came from the Light and they will return to the Light** in a short period of time. Their return will not be through the death process of the physical body, as it has been for eons. Make them aware that this body is only temporary, and they will remove it when they move into the Light and return **Home** to the Spirit World. When we say **soon**, this is in Spirit time... for we know you will be measuring it in Earth time. There is still a little while until everything is ready for the ascension of your planet.

There are many advanced souls amongst you; beings of light who have finally awakened and are spreading their wings, making the necessary changes in their lives. They will slowly remember what they came to do on the Planet. As their **spiritual gifts** unfold, they will consciously know what part they chose to play in the Divine scheme. They will **know** that all is in Divine Order in their lives and that it is the beginning of their new life, performing the tasks they chose before their incarnation.

You are living in the **Time of Revelations** when old information is being released. Much is brought forth to awaken the soul to allow the information which has laid dormant for eons to surface. The **DNA strands**, your connection to the Spirit World, are being reconnected. We are aware of the fear and the negativity caused by that fear; but as you begin to let go and let God be in charge of your life, you move into your **Higher Self.** Each day will be like a new beginning.

An Awakening Humanity

To help you to awaken, a new awareness is surfacing from the soul as it is needed, a little at a time. Some of you cannot absorb the large amount of information coming through at once, and it will be easier to understand and accept in smaller quantities. Your energy field will change, and the density disappear from your vibration as you begin to remember, understand, and believe.

We want you to know that we are very close to you, and that we are working with you. Your guardian angels are with you; they are always there for you when you need them. As you become more aware of their Divine presence, you will awaken to whom you truly are as the soul.

You are in a country at this moment where much growth is needed. (I was in Costa Rica). These people are like little children, but they have their faith. They put their trust in God, and they live their faith to a certain degree. This is enough for some of them... they do not need more information than that. As Christ said two thousand years ago, *"Unless ye become like little children, ye cannot enter the Kingdom of Heaven."* They believe in the Power and Love of a God who is taking care of them, and will take them where they are to be when the time is right. It is important that they be allowed to continue doing this for the time being. There are those who will not awaken at this point in time, but do not worry about them. They will be able to cross into the Light as quickly as anyone else if they have deep faith in their Beloved God.

Your world cannot stay the same, because you are living in the time of *Endings and New Beginnings;* both are important. As you move forward with the spirituality that is growing within you, and your body becomes lighter as you move into the Ascension energy, you will realize that you need less Earthly food. Through your meditations, you will receive the energy that is needed to keep your body balanced and in perfect health.

Because of the termination of karma on Planet Earth, many things are shaking up in the lives of each of you. When you find the inner strength to take the steps necessary to make the changes in your lives, awareness will begin to seep in, and your soul will once again take its rightful place in your life.

Do not try to force others to understand prematurely; they will awaken in their own time. It is their divine right to be where they are, and you can only share your knowledge and your love with other souls whom you sense might be ready. Share your spiritual knowledge with them only to the degree they can understand; sometimes one phrase at a time. If they are going through devastating experiences in their own lives, encourage them and give them love; do not take on their karma. Give them **unconditional love,** knowing that they will work through these problems, and the results will be for their highest good. Sometimes the road may be bumpy, but they will emerge from their journey with the soul growth that was needed.

Be aware of the children, for these little beings are so important to Planet Earth. They come direct from **The Source** to help you understand unconditional love. Many of them are only here temporarily to help awaken humanity, and they will return to our side in just a few years. No matter how difficult the life experience they were coming into was to be for them, they were very happy to be a part of the great **Cosmic Experience** that is taking place on Planet Earth. On a soul level they remembered that they *chose* to be an instrument, not only for the growth of the family, but for many others who heard

An Awakening Humanity ~117

about and wept at the experiences they went through, whether they were negative or positive.

Some people only learn from negative experiences. That is all right, because many will receive soul growth when they hear of the trauma the little children are going through at this moment. Know that it is only temporary, and that changes are taking place. Be aware of how the news of these experiences turn people towards God; even if it is only to ask, "Where are you, God? Why are you allowing this to happen?" You know, beloved ones, that God does not *allow* anything to happen... it is there as an experience for the soul, which it *chose* to help humanity in their awakening process.

It is important to keep balanced and grounded most of the time so that you may be aware of all that is happening around you. At the same time, those amongst you who are truly awakening, must work more on their ascension process. Release the density of the physical body through meditation. As you relax in your chair, feel the density of your physical body completely disappearing. As you sit there in your astral body, be aware of **being pure Light**. By doing this exercise every day, you will move forward much faster in your growth.

Go into your Light bodies during your meditation periods, and allow it to move out to heal those in need of physical, mental or emotional healing. See your Light body working at a distance on someone whom you know needs healing. What some would call *miracle* healing is performed through you, and you will realize the Divine power that is there for your utilization. These are new energies for healing, working through the Light body, that have been given to the planet.

You are **Spiritual Beings**, and you may use your astral or Light body, which is a replica of your physical body, to do healings in any part of the world. At this moment in time, the energy is very powerful and the techniques are easy to learn. Wherever you are sitting, go into a deep state of meditation. Visualize your spiritual or Light body moving out of your physical body and going to the person who has requested healing. Practice these techniques, working on the areas of the body that are afflicted. If you sense that their dis-ease is caused by a need to transmute situations in their lives, just surround them with the Violet Light, that the transmutation process may go forth. You will not believe the results you will have!

Teach these techniques to others, because they must also learn to use these new and powerful energies. With all the changes taking place on the planet, there is a great need for healing, especially for the emotional body. Each must learn to balance this body by detaching from the situations in their lives that need to be released. They may then move into the spiritual work many of them came to do – the important tasks chosen before incarnating. You must help them to understand the need for detachment from situations around them, replacing the energy with unconditional love in all circumstances. They need to practice it as often as possible, until they really understand the concept and it becomes second nature to them.

The animals around you need your help. They are very important to the balance in the world, as they bring much love. Their vibrations are changing, and on a certain level they know what is happening. As you give them more love and understanding, accepting that they are part of Divine energy and have their purpose, you will open your own heart; the cruelty that they are experiencing will stop. They are there to love you and to teach you to love, but they need your help.

Open your heart to God's special little creatures and let them feel your love for them. Let them know that they are important, accepting that they are part of the Divine energy as much as you are, and that they have their place in the universe as much as you do.

We want you to know that you are much loved and can contact us at will. Just sit down, open your heart and listen to the still small voice within. By learning to meditate, you can quiet the mind and open the heart. Call on us to help you as you move into the new energy that is permeating the planet. We know that you all sense it and have noticed the changes in the weather patterns – the storms and the earthquakes which are beginning to accelerate in many areas of your world. This will make you question what is happening on the planet, and **why** it is happening. They are there to awaken you to your Divinity, that you may understand that you can change the weather patterns. They do not need to be as devastating as some of them are. You have created this through your negative energy, the energy of your thoughts and deeds that have gone into the ethers and remained around the planet. This energy accumulates and comes back to you as storms, hurricanes, even causing volcanoes to erupt.

If you start projecting loving energy out into the universe instead, these **catastrophes**, could be reversed to a certain degree. Mankind will not become perfect overnight. Some lessons are needed, but the devastation can be lessened if each of you do your share by keeping your thoughts loving and harmonious every moment of the day. In the old energy pattern, if you expected negative things to happen, they always did. You attracted to yourselves whatever you put out in mental energy, the Natural Law of Cause and Effect was always prevalent... *as ye sow, so shall ye reap.*

It is important for you to understand that this concept is no longer relevant; there are no more lessons for you to learn, as karma is finished on Planet Earth. If all the Earth children keep their thoughts and deeds loving at all times, and function permanently through the **Higher Self,** they will truly *bring Heaven down on Earth, as it was originally meant to be.*

We love you... I am St.-Germain

CHAPTER NINE

MOTHER EARTH AND HER INHABITANTS

ARCHANGEL GABRIEL

Eons ago, before time as you now know it, we existed as Archangels and we had our designated tasks in many areas in the Universes.

Planet Earth was a star when the Creator decided to try a new experiment. We were all happy to participate in this Divine plan. It was like birthing a new baby and watching it grow in wisdom, bringing forth what was to be a vast project different from anything that had ever been tried before. The creativity involved for the magnitude of this project implicated millions of souls from our side. When it began, there were no **humans,** as this species evolved over millions of years.

The original plan for Earth was to create a new system whereby the souls who incarnated there would have free will. The new law of *Cause and Effect,* which gave each soul the right to make their decisions (**cause**), and have to live with the consequence (**effect**), would reign supreme. This new endeavor would allow them to acquire *soul growth* through each of their incarnations on Planet Earth. By following the *Spiritual Laws* which were inherent their soul would receive the needed growth. If instead, they listened to their egos and chose experiences which were detrimental to their soul, they would regress. At some point, the positive and negative experiences chosen over all their earthly incarnations had to be balanced.

You reincarnated with various souls with whom you had shared many lifetimes. Each return was an attempt to balance the **karma,** debt owed by you to another or by another soul to you, due to the wrongs that had been done in other lifetimes. You could return in a male or female body, depending on the gender needed for the karmic patterns you were working out.

Each of you have interacted in previous lives with your family members and those around you in this lifetime. There are moments when you meet someone for the first time and feel as if you have known them forever! This instantaneous connection felt is caused by **soul recognizing soul,** and is usually the result of two souls who have been together and deeply loved each other in many incarnations. Sometimes they are permitted to come back at the same time as a compensation for work well done in other lifetimes. There is no love more powerful than that between two souls who are intertwined through a spiritual, as well as a physical love vibration. They are sometimes referred to as **soul mates.** They can often read each other's mind, or sense if one of them is in danger. This can be any relationship: husband and wife, father or mother with a child, brother and sister, even loving friends of either gender.

Gradually things began to change as the Earth children forgot they were Spiritual Beings, and permitted their **egos** and **lower selves** to control their lives. As they moved further and further away from the Light, the density of the energy field on and around the planet began to change. They were moving away from the original plan which was to bring Heaven down on Earth.

Over eons, as the energy on Earth changed, the density moved into the consciousness of the souls inhabiting the planet. Their way of thinking changed drastically until, at some point, many of them completely forgot that they had originally come from the Light. The more evolved souls never wavered in their faith, and always remembered their Spiritual heritage. They returned to Earth over and over to help others to remember, but the negative energy invaded the minds of the vast majority. The Spiritual truths were forgotten and the task of trying to turn them around became more and more difficult. At some point the all powerful ego had taken control of too man, and a division was made between different factions, each forming their own religion. Each group thought theirs was the best, and tried to force others to believe as they did. They made their own rules as they went along, trying to control the vast majority of souls by convincing them that they had all the answers.

When mankind fell away from the Light and moved towards Earthly pleasures they fell into darkness and cut their connection with the God energy. There was always a little voice inside which tried to tell them they were on the wrong path but they refused to listen. Finally they no longer felt this connection with their soul and their Divine heritage and functioned completely from the ego.

The Spiritual Law of Cause and Effect had been in force since the beginning, and they became their own worst enemy. They refused to heed the still small voice in their heart which was telling them they were off the pathway and heading for destruction if they did not turn their life around.

Through the Law of Cause and Effect they attracted to themselves many varieties of illnesses to help them realize the destructive pattern they were following. Many did not want to understand, however, for they were enjoying their new way of thinking and Earthly pleasures. Many were drawn into pagan rituals, which turned them away from God. Instead they began to worship idols which were not of the Light. They moved towards a negative energy from which they had great difficulty extracting themselves if they changed their minds, because the leaders were working with the dark forces on the planet.

Please believe me when I say that life was not always easy at the beginning, because these souls had never known anything but **Light.** It was difficult to go to a new world, and have choices to make in every area of their lives. They had accepted, and were very excited to be a part of this experiment on Planet Earth, but didn't realize the difficulties having to make choices would entail. Some learned through their errors, and often vacillated over decision making for long periods in their struggle with the ego. For many the ego always won in the long run.

There came a time when a cleansing was needed on the planet. The human race had moved so far from the original Spiritual teachings that they became **inhuman.** Mankind had become far too powerful for its own good, and the good of all Humanity.

On two occasions, flooding the Earth was the vehicle for the needed lesson. These two cataclysms went down in your history books as the sinking of Lemuria and Atlantis. They were very important events, as it was God's way of giving his precious children a second chance through a clearing and a cleansing of the planet; one more time to start anew.

A certain number of evolved souls who had incarnated on the planet at that time were saved. They were there for that purpose... to start a new world and a new race of people. God was giving His children another chance. ***The original experiment***

with the Natural and Spiritual Laws on the planet was not yet over.

Now is the time when the experiment is ended. Karma as you knew it is now terminated! The world is changing... many new things will be taking place on the planet. Things you may not understand at the beginning will become clearer as you advance on your pathway. They are there for your growth, dear ones... the growth of your soul.

Many of you are very advanced souls, but you do not yet know or remember this. Soon the awareness will surface and new doors will open for you; you shall be moving onto new pathways. The right people will be put on your path, to give you the information needed to trigger the changes that are about to take place in your lives, through the soul's awakening. Do not fear... nothing necessary shall be taken from your lives and all changes are for your highest good.

Many around you are awakening to who they truly are as the soul. Some who are moving onto their Spiritual pathway have been through great traumas, not only in this lifetime, but in many others. The memories of these traumatic times are surfacing to be cleared and cleansed, but they do not understand this. As their souls awaken, they will often feel the need to cry, as the tears are close to the surface. Everything is being released from the subconscious mind.

Many physical problems will be healed through the releasing of the blockages caused by experiences in past lifetimes; sometimes several in a row, which have carried over into this incarnation. You will think that everything is falling apart around you, and you may feel a state of depression like you have possibly never felt before in your life. Your soul is trying to tell you that you are **off the pathway, or a new pathway is opening for you –** and you must move forward onto it.

Never fear, you will have all the help that you require – you need only *to let go and let God.* You need to surrender to the energy that is there and let the tears flow. They are cleansing your subconscious mind of all that is there. Release... please allow those tears to flow; do not feel that you are falling into a state of depression and worry about it. It is the opposite; this depression is what is triggering the clearing and cleansing that needs to surface at this time. It is time to be released. If you accept it as a needed experience, you will start to feel lighter and lighter. There is no need for you to consciously know what experience in which lifetime is being released, for some may be too traumatic for you to re-live on a conscious level. You need only thank God for the releasing at this moment, as each time a part of those buried memories surface to be cleared, you will move another step forward on your pathway. You will feel that your physical body is lighter, that a load you were carrying has been taken from you. It will be like **crying a bucket of tears,** as you sometimes say, but know they are cleansing tears; bless them and let them flow.

It will be more difficult for the males to allow themselves to show emotions they have hidden all their lives, as pride will come into play. Those around them who are more evolved, must help them to express those emotions. Assure them it is a natural part of the process of cleansing the emotional body. At the same time they are clearing from their subconscious minds the debris of all of their incarnations. Tell them it is important that the tears be permitted to flow; that this is a healing that has been needed for a long time. If need be, hold them in your arms as a mother would hold her child. This may also help in your own understanding and forgiveness of the things that transpired in the karma working out between souls – possibly yourself and another. It was only a karmic lesson. It will be replaced by a new understanding of what is taking place on an entirely different level in the lives of each of you. You will never be the same again, or want to walk back into that old life, as moments of joy like none you have ever known, surface from the core of your being. You will feel that a heaviness you seemed to have carried forever has disappeared and your step will be lighter. The unshed tears took a lot of emotional space and were a heavy burden to carry, possibly causing emotional and physical problems. You will feel lighter – as if a spiritual awakening is making room for your soul to take its proper place in your life as the captain of your ship.

Be aware of those around you who need your help. They are having difficulties awakening, as they may not be as spiritually evolved as you are. You need to help each other. Lend a helping hand on the pathway to awareness, as you walk side by side, supporting one another through the problems you are each going through in your own way. The advancement will be much faster for both as your energy field will be raised through the helping hand you will give others. You always feel good when you help other, and there is a great need for that at this moment. Be a good listener; they can get a better perspective of what is happening in their lives by bringing their worries to the surface and taking a better look at them. If they ask you for advice, do so in a loving way with no recriminations about the past. Many of them will already be feeling guilt as all the negative attitudes will surface for them to become aware of their existence. Assure them that everything happens for a reason; then tell them to close the door on the past and move forward taking one step at a time into the new life that will be opening to them.

It is time to return to praying. It is still as powerful as it always has been. Let your memory take you back to the time as a little child when you got on your knees before going to sleep each night. Do you remember how important those moments were to the little soul whose memories of his or her life in the Spirit World before incarnating may still have been close to the surface? Go back to the prayers and the invocations... thank God for everything good and bad that is happening in your life. The faster this is done the sooner you will move onto your new pathway. The doors will open for you left and right. New friends and fellow travelers will be put on your path and it will be a joyful time.

When you look back over the last few years you probably wonder how you got through all the upheavals in every area of your lives. You will always come through each challenge much stronger, however, if you look for the Light rather than the darkness. Put forgiveness and unconditional love in every situation accepting that it was for your highest good.

Be aware of the little ones, as much is happening in their world today. As Mankind changes and turns towards God, they will become loving parents once again. In the meantime the children are suffering. Give them a loving pat on the head as you walk by them and surround them with love and light. Many of the children born over the past few years are very advanced beings. They are also remembering who they truly are as the soul, and what their destiny path is. It is very important that you teach them to pray to Mary, their Divine

Mother in Heaven, whose task is to love and care for the children. Ask for Her blessing on your precious little ones.

The world is moving from the darkness to the Light. It took mankind eons to go from Light into darkness, and now you are turning back, reversing the flow of energy on the planet. It will get easier as the understanding of what is happening gradually seeps into the subconscious mind and then to the conscious mind. This is why it is important to permit your Higher Self to control your life. Once you have awakened do not let anyone sway you in your decision to listen to the important advice that is coming from deep inside of you. In your heart you will always know the right step to take in each situation. It will never lead you astray.

The dawning of each day brings new growth for you. Wake up in the morning with anticipation of the wonderful things each day will bring. Expect the best and the highest from the changes that will be brought into your life and the new people who will be put on your pathway; and you shall receive them. Never allow any negativity to penetrate your aura. If it does, say the word *cancel*, and the negative thought will immediately disappear from your energy field. This is only the past that is still cleansing and clearing – do not dwell on the negative in your past when there is nothing you can change. You will become stronger as you keep moving forward into the light. As you grow spiritually accept who you are and start living as that soul; you will feel as if you are ten feet tall.

We are close to you, and sometimes bring much information in the sleep state. Bits and pieces will seep into the conscious mind during the day – allow it to happen without questioning. This information is needed for whatever area of your life to which it pertains.

You must learn to love unconditionally, giving everyone the right to be who they are, until they too awaken and reach their full soul potential. No one is better than another; you are each in the place you are meant to be at this point in time. Recriminations and judgment must be completely released. Speak to everyone lovingly; tell them you are there to help them if they need to talk or whatever.

Many souls on your planet feel so alone! They feel that no one understands them, and they move deeper and deeper inside themselves. At some point an experience in their life will take them to the bottom. This must happen to bring forth the tears to clear and cleanse the situations that need to be reversed. They must realize and accept what they cannot change; they can only modify the way they perceive the situation. You usually get the most soul growth during situations in your lives when you touch bottom.

We know how difficult it is to clear the emotional body, but it must be done to become completely balanced. It is then that situations will start changing in your lives. You will be led every step of the way because your answers will come from inside yourselves rather than searching outside. The answers come from the still small voice, or your intuition, which is your soul telling you what is right for you – which step to take – what decision to make. As you begin to listen more and more you will instantly know where you need to be at certain times in your lives.

It is a wonderful world out there! Become little children, for you are just beginning your lives. The past is over; you are a changed being. The remembrance of who you are as the soul will surface little by little, giving you more assurance. Begin practicing unconditional love for self, for you must do this before you can love others unconditionally.

Mother Earth and Her Inhabitants ~131

God is eternally close to you. To feel this closeness, you must talk to Him/Her as you would a loving friend. Mother Mary is also close to the planet and working with each soul who requests her help. Send up your thoughts and your prayers to the ethers. Ask them for help and protection for yourself, your loved ones and friends. They must await your request as you still have free will. Your angels are around you for protection and guidance; sense them standing behind your shoulder watching over you, protecting you, and guiding you with love. With this feeling of protection in your heart... ***knowing*** that they are always there for you, things will change very quickly in your life. You will not allow any fear or negative thoughts to enter as they cancel the positive ones. Come out of the dark... it is now time to move into the light where you belong. We are close to you, we are there for you; you need only to call on us.

As you move forward with a new sense of inner peace, you will know that you are living in a new world. As mankind goes through its changes, it is important to understand the period of growth that is also there for the planet – changes that are taking place in every area.

The devastating events occurring on Earth at this time may make you think that humanity is becoming more corrupt, but it is not so. The darkness is being replaced by the Light. Everything is surfacing for you to realize how far the Earth children have strayed from their original beginnings as Spiritual beings.

Nothing can remain hidden any longer, **the Light is shining in every corner of the Earth.** Each situation that needs changing on your planet is surfacing to be cleared and cleansed and put into the Light. How are you to know what is being done in secrecy behind the scenes, unless it surfaces for you to realize that it is there? You may think, "what terrible things these are!" Yes, dear children, they are terrible things; but this makes you realize how low much of humanity has sunk. Take comfort in knowing that you are finally moving into the Light and each situation that surfaces will be cleared and cleansed and gone forever.

The hunger for power and the greed in most of the governments and institutions in your world must no longer be permitted. If decisions are not made for the **Highest Good** of the majority of the people they must be changed or eliminated. Those of you who have the capabilities must stand tall and take the necessary steps to help make the changes even if it is only speaking out against injustices. For those who are unable to get involved directly surround it with Light and *know* that it is already taken care of. No matter how negative it may seem, view it in a Spiritual sense. Think of the good that will come from this, as each situation is turned into positive action. Many evolved souls are already in place in every government on the planet ready to take their responsibilities as loving beings who want only the highest good, not only for the few, but for all of Humanity. This mission was chosen by these souls before incarnating, whether or not they remember it at this point in time. All situations are surrounded with Light from **Loving Beings** from our side.

The souls that have chosen to return to Spirit at this time unconsciously made that choice long ago, and their passing will often trigger the awakening of many souls on the planet. The more devastating the experience, the more souls will be touched by it – especially if the passing involves children. Even though we know this is usually beyond your comprehension on a conscious level, there are times you just have to trust in a higher power, knowing that everything is in Divine Order.

You will see many changes in the weather patterns over the next few years. This is necessary to cleanse the planet of the negativity that was created by mankind's thought patterns. You didn't understand that every negative thought that you had went out into the ethers and stayed there! This negativity accumulated for long periods and came back to you as thunderstorms, tornadoes, hurricanes, etc. Devastating things for humanity – but they are part of the Natural Law of Cause and Effect. Each of you helped create this and now all is being released through the strange weather patterns producing bizarre weather in all parts of the world. There is always good that comes out of something negative – remember this. So when you see what is happening out there, do not feel fear of any kind. Send light out into the ethers and ask your guardian angels for protection.

Following a few years of cleansing the atmosphere around the planet things will settle down. Mother Earth will be making her Ascension, and you will be ascending with her. By then you will be changed beings; you will not recognize yourselves or the Earth. Everyone on the planet will have moved into the Light – with new thought forms and a new way of thinking. By having love in your hearts for yourselves and everyone else and finally understanding the Natural and Spiritual Laws of the Universe, ***you will finally be bringing Heaven down on Earth.***

I am Archangel Gabriel and I Bless Each Of You!

CHAPTER TEN

POWER OF LOVE

SANANDA

Love is the most powerful vibration in the Universe! Through love all is possible. Until you have known love, you have not known life. Many of the family and friends that surround you do not know how to love; this is something that must be learned. It is very important to every aspect of your lives. Through love you will have health and happiness. Loving in the proper way makes your life fulfilling, enabling you to help others around you to get on their pathway.

You can receive a healing just by being close to someone who is working strongly on a love vibration, and who has come full circle in his knowledge as the soul. All that is needed is the desire that your life be changed to the degree that you can know happiness as you want it, and all will be done for you.

The energy around you will completely change. Some people will disappear from your life because they will not be able to be close to the love vibration, if they have not learned to love themselves. Their own negativity will be their greatest teacher, as they will touch bottom in some way to bring them to the culmination point where they will realize that they **need** and want love in their lives. They will want to be loving people, doing for others rather than expecting others to do for them.

Too many people on Earth depend on others for their happiness! This is not possible, dear children; you must give love in order to receive it. There were periods during your childhood when you felt you didn't receive love. These were due to blockages from past lives and in your current life, which made it difficult for you to understand, and kept you from knowing how to request it.

You only need to open to that love and reciprocate, usually starting in a family situation where the parents and siblings are loving. This carries over into their everyday lives, touching everyone around them and assisting in altering many things that need to be changed in themselves. This is achieved by learning to love themselves.

Through love you will be living in the Divine vibration and the knowledge will flow through you into your physical body and your soul. This will help you to understand every moment of your lives. Allow the loving being you truly are to surface, accepting others as they are, no matter what is happening around them or what they are doing.

Unconditional love prevails at this point in time on the planet. You must learn to use it every moment of your day, understanding that others are going through their traumas as they awaken as the soul. The unawakened ones are being bombarded by the energy of love which is coming from our side. It is also being projected by the souls who have awakened and are performing their tasks as Lightworkers for the Divine Energy, serving on the planet to awaken others. The love flows from them and breaks through the hardest shells when the time is right. Keep yourselves in the vibration of unconditional love and project this love to those who need it. They will help themselves if they are ready to understand. Love can melt the hardest hearts! The only reason these hearts are hard is because they have gone through many incarnations lacking love.

Be aware of those around you who are suffering greatly because of their lack of love. There is much help needed in this domain. Know that this is part of the task that you have chosen in this lifetime. You are moving into the time when everything is changing on Earth. As the vibratory rate is raised and the energy of unconditional love permeates the planet, know that those of you who have awakened are very blessed; there is much work for you to do as you go forth on your new pathway.

You have overcome much, dear children of Light, coming through the awakening period with needed growth. Now all is in place for you to go forward, moving with grace, into this new life. Many endeavors await you. Know that we are close to you for any help that you might need – you only have to ask, and we are there.

As you awaken the vibration of unconditional love, you will realize that your whole life will change. You will be living in the *Now*, not in the past or in the future. You will be living in your heart, receiving your answers from your **Higher Self** each moment of every day. You must understand that the answers are always there waiting for you... but you must ask for them.

As you move more and more into the understanding of the love vibration, you will constantly be aware that you only have to listen to the *still small voice* in your heart to receive all of your answers. You will know immediately what is right or what is wrong for you. Your **Higher Self,** which has finally come into its own and reached the culmination point where it can be of service to you at every moment, will not steer you wrong. The only mistakes you will make will be through your refusal to listen to what it is telling you, either through a voice in your mind or in your heart. Through the understanding and acceptance that whatever is happening will be for your **highest good,** you will **know** that this inner voice will not lead you astray; you will continually listen to the advice and messages it brings you.

You ***must be aware*** of living in the now... that your mind is stilled so that you may always hear the small voice giving you your answers. By always being aware that your **Higher Self** is directing your life, and realizing that each decision is right, you will have more and more confidence and trust in yourself and your inner voice. You will refuse to make decisions without getting the answers from your soul, rather than listening to the ego and the mind. That is where the mistakes are made.

By learning to love yourselves unconditionally, you will become aware of who you are. The answers that are given to you will always be the right ones, and will save you from many actions that could cause you to deviate from your Spiritual pathway. If you deviate from your path following a long period of allowing the soul to direct your lives, you will realize how unstable your situations have become. Nothing is working in your life anymore, because once again you have made the mistake of turning your back on your **Higher Self**. As you progress and learn to love yourself more and more, this will happen less frequently. There will come a time when every moment of your day will be directed by the loving soul that you are, and you will know what is right for you.

Staying in this love vibration will enable you to be of service to others around you, guiding them in making their decisions through answers you receive from **your Higher Self**.

This is only a temporary measure, however, until you can teach them to love themselves enough to take the steps that you took when you moved forward on your new pathway into the mission you came to Earth to perform in this incarnation.

Out of love, you may try to help others. Understand, though, that they are still responsible for themselves. If they do not wish to listen to your advice, even if it is what they need, they must be free to make their own decisions and continue making their own mistakes. Once they understand that they are not on the correct path, they will turn themselves around, and very slowly start to progress in their own soul growth. By learning to quiet the mind, they also may hear the ***still small voice*** in their heart.

You will help many people, but there are those that are not ready for the love that you have to give. Members of your own families may not understand you, and will not be ready to make the changes necessary for their own soul growth. This is all right. Everyone has the right to be at the stage they are, and you cannot push them into something for which they are not ready. Time is short, so do not waste it trying to force someone to understand. Each soul will awaken in its own time.

Stay calm when they make mistakes, and give them a loving example of no recriminations. They will err less and less as they walk down their spiritual pathway and final awakening, realizing how you and others around them are happy and fulfilled in the work you are doing – the work that, as the soul, you came to Earth in this incarnation to do.

More and more spiritual beings will be put on your pathway. You will sense the vibration as being of a family member, even though they are not your Earthly family. Many

soul mates and ***twin flames*** are coming together in love... your spiritual families are drawing close to you, and it is very important that you stay open to this fact. When you meet someone and feel as if you have always known this person soulwise, realize that they are on your path for a reason; there is a purpose for them being with you at this moment. Keep in touch with them until you know what and where you are supposed to be in each others lives. There may be some spiritual work that you are destined to do together, which shall be revealed to both of you in time. Stay close to the people with whom you feel a very strong love vibration. It may sometimes feel like a brotherly or sisterly love, or you may feel as if they are your mother or father. Possibly they **were** in a past life, and they are to be part of your spiritual family in this lifetime, allowing all of you to move forward in the new endeavors which are waiting for you, and which you have each chosen before this incarnation.

Understand that much joy will be brought to you, and this joy must be shared with others. Project this vibration of joy to others whom you feel are depressed, and see if it helps them. They must accept that ultimately they must help themselves by learning self love. Earth children are only now beginning to understand its importance. During the many incarnations you have had, you were taught the opposite. Know that the truth is now coming to the forefront; you are spiritual beings, and it is important that you love yourselves so that you may sow this love to everyone who needs it.

As you climb the new stairs for the work into which you each will be going, you must climb one step at a time, taking time to ground each new situation in your life. You are still living on the planet, and there is a need for the grounding in every aspect of your spiritual work.

Prepare the time you need to rest and relax, spending time with loving friends. Spiritual mates will be working with you, and supporting you as you support others. You will recognize your spiritual family; do not be surprised that it is rather large. Each time you meet someone that you *feel in the very core of your being that you have always known*, accept that this is a soul mate, someone who has been in your life over and over, as you developed your spiritual gifts in other lifetimes as well. Now is the time for the true awakening and all the doors will open unto you.

Don't be afraid of anything that is happening around you; know that you are protected, and you will always be in the right place at the right time. As we have said, *listen to the still small voice in your heart giving you the right answers.* Do not make decisions without first consulting your higher or spiritual self, so that no time is wasted and you do not have to backtrack.

There will come a time when you will know immediately what is right for you. Lessons will no longer be necessary once you understand who you truly are, and what you came here to do as the soul.

Do not expect everything to unfold at one time! There will be pieces here and there, doors that will be opening for you. Many people will be put on your pathway to help you. This will be done in a way that you will be able to deal with each situation as it comes up. Positive and loving situations will help you take each step forward into the new work in which you will be going.

As you learn to *become* unconditional love, the souls will sense your energy field which will have expanded to encompass a great distance around you. Often they will not know what is happening to them as they step into your Light essence, but something is being triggered, and an awakening will take place. They will make the choice whether they wish to go forward and follow through with all of the new ideas flowing into their mind. Once it enters the mind, they will learn to listen with their heart and soul and decide whether it is for their highest good.

There is no weakness in anyone... only hidden strength which has not yet surfaced. Many have been through devastating times which has brought their physical energy level down, even to the point of having what you call nervous or mental breakdowns. Often they must go through this crucial experience to grow, to finally awaken by having gone to the depths of despair – knowing **there is nowhere else to go but up**. That is when they will finally reach out, and search for the help and the love that they need to awaken to their Divinity. You will be there waiting for them, and you will recognize when they are ready. You must utilize your power of love with them, and listen to what they have to tell you. This is very important to their healing and their burgeoning soul growth, moving them onto the new pathway that awaits them. They will realize that they do not ever want to regress, or go through another traumatic experience like the one they just came out of. They have no choice but to look in the opposite direction towards the positive energy of love and joy. They will want positive people around them, moving away from the negative people with whom they had always been friends, because – **like attracts like**. Now they are ready for a new life, and you must be there to help them. Keep them surrounded in Light and love, but do not let them siphon your energy or bring down your Light. Surround them with the Violet Ray for transmutation. Teach them to use this for themselves, bringing it down through the crown chakra and into their body, that the stress and all negativity in their cells be released. New cells will form with the loving energy that will be there for them as their soul awakens. Listen to them, but do not feel pity. Tell them who they are and that God loves them; that they must learn to love themselves as much as their Heavenly Father does! Tell them that they are Divine beings who came from the Light and who will return to the Light! There is no other way that they can recover from these devastating situations except to move towards the Light, because the energy on the planet is changing. All of the experiences are being brought to the surface for the Light to be put on them, that they may be transmuted through the Violet Ray and the Violet Flame, into perfect Light and perfect Love.

Sometimes the most advanced Beings on the planet have been through devastating things in their lives, coming out triumphant because they persisted. They somehow *knew* that there was something else, possibly a new way of life that they had to find – they searched until they found it. At times they felt as if they were drowning in deep water and, as they broke through the surface and came into the radiance of the Light, they knew that something in them had changed. Something had been *triggered* by that negative experience... possibly over a period of years of alcohol or drug addiction which is so devastating to the mind, body and soul. Sometimes they needed to go through a ***Near Death Experience***, to go to the very door or portals of the Other Side to realize what they have done to themselves and their body... this magnificent physical body which the Beloved Father/Mother God gave them through which to function, that they might grow as the soul and realize their Divinity.

Many of you realize subconsciously that this is your last incarnation on Planet Earth, and your final chance for soul growth. Now is the time when everything must be brought to the surface to be cleared and cleansed that you may move into the Light. Many of your most evolved souls on Earth at this point in time have been through many devastating experiences. Even though they will share how difficult it was – to the magnitude that they sometimes questioned whether they would survive the experience – now realize that it was because of this that they learned to love themselves, and now they can love others. Through the sharing of their own experiences, others who are living what seems to them their **Hell on Earth,** can lift themselves up by hanging on to God. This may only be a figure of speech to them, as they may never have known Him in this lifetime for some reason or another. Possibly they did not want to know Him, or were never taught the importance this Supreme Being should have had in their lives. But the experiences *needed* will be given to them, no matter how devastating they are. They will grow from them and *come into the Light,* and learn to love.

They are the ones who will step forward after their healing and help others who are going through similar experiences. They might help the children, as they realize that many of their problems as an unloved child were a result of their choice to be born into a family situation that led to these experiences. You *always chose your experiences,* dear children, remember this! Do not blame anyone around you; they are all players on *your stage of life,* and most of these souls were known to you in other incarnations. You chose your experiences and them, as you wanted to finish up some karmic patterns which were there from other lifetimes.

Know that you are very blessed that you go through these traumatic times, as this is when you receive the most soul growth. Accept this and move into the Light, putting the past behind you, thanking God for having given you these experiences. Know that if you had not gone through them, you would not know the joy of *unconditional love*. The joy of unconditional love that you have for yourself and for others – you finally *know who you are!*

Respect and love yourselves as much as your Beloved Father loves you. Never forget that you are His children. He is always waiting with open arms to welcome you back into the fold of the Heavenly family, after having learned the hard lessons that were needed for you to become the Divine Light Being that you truly are. We want you to know that we love you dearly! We are there for you at every moment, you only have to call on us.

Look towards a wonderful future, a time when you will *know who you truly are as a Divine Being.* You will finally understand how blessed you are to be on the planet... to be living through these wonderful times, as you move forward towards the *Ascension of Mother Earth,* and the new beginnings that will take place for each of you. We Bless you... we bring you much love. Many Beings are standing here waiting for you to hold out your hand and *ask* for the help that you need. Remember *first and foremost* that you must learn to love yourselves unconditionally, understanding and accepting that there was a purpose for each experience that you went through–that purpose was : *For the growth of the soul, and to learn to love yourself and others as much as God loves you!.*

We Bless you!

CHAPTER ELEVEN

RELEASING PAST THOUGHT PATTERNS

1996 is the year when we can Ascend out of our old reality of lack and limitation and into our new reality of Heaven on Earth. To accomplish this, we must totally change our perception of life, and accept that we are the beloved children of our Divine Father/Mother God. He/She wants each of us to have abundance and prosperity in every domain. This has been part of our Divine heritage from the beginning of time; but how can we understand this concept if we have never learned to love ourselves? We have been on a guilt trip for two thousand years, being told that we were unworthy, therefore undeserving of God's love or abundance. The teachings over that time should have been the message that Christ brought to the Earth 2000 years ago, the most important part being... *that we were the children of a loving Father in Heaven who only wanted the best for us.* Instead we were told that we were worthless and condemned to God's punishment, unless we adhered to **their** belief system. With the elevation of the vibrations on the planet, and the awakening to their Divinity of millions of souls who are moving onto a new Spiritual pathway, everything is changing. Each of us is now able to receive our answers from our *Higher Selves* which continually tells us **"You are worthy, you are loved... and you must love yourself as much as God loves you."**

Because of the changes in the energy field and the ending of karma in 1995 all manifestations are direct. It no longer takes years for our actions to have reactions. **What we sow today through our thoughts, words, or deeds, we reap**

tomorrow. Therefore it is important to always keep our thoughts loving and positive. The fact that karma has ended on the planet only changes the Law of Cause and Effect to the degree that we are no longer working out **past life** karma. We are still responsible for our day to day thoughts and deeds. We cannot have negative attitudes towards everyone and all situations, and not expect that the repercussions from this negativity will manifest in other ways. If we persist in continuing in this vein of thought and actions, we can produce illness in our physical bodies. What a wonderful world it would be if we smiled at everyone we met, as if we were seeing an old friend.

When I go into stores or public places, I sometimes sense the inner turmoil that is going on in the lives of some of the people I meet. I try to keep a smiling face, especially for those that I know from their vibrations are going through personal traumas. Sometimes I will move onto their path just to give them a smile, or compliment them in some way. I immediately feel a shift in their whole vibration... as if I've touched a lonely place deep in their heart that they realize only a stranger could find. One thoughtful gesture such as this could turn a stranger's whole life around. For one brief moment they felt that **someone cared**.

Living in the *Now* means to be focused on what is happening in our lives at every moment. Not thinking of yesterday, or worrying about tomorrow! It's having a wonderful sense of **inner knowing** that everything in our lives is in Divine Order. We have the utmost faith that God is taking care of us, and our needs will be met in every area. It means releasing all fear, and continually staying in what can only be described as a balanced state. It is a state of being where we are constantly in touch with our Higher Self and can receive the answers we need to function in our daily lives.

When we are no longer under the domination of our ego, there is no more duality. It becomes easier to hear that ***still small voice*** giving us the right answers. At the beginning, they may be received through a feeling to take or not take a certain action, or to cancel some plan we had made. If the feeling is subtle but persistent, and seems to be coming from somewhere inside yourself rather than your mind, it is important to heed this. As you learn to listen to the information coming from the core of your being, you will always know instantly whether something is right or not for you. We sometimes called this our **intuition,** and some considered it a special power that many were given at birth. It is also considered a spiritual gift and, if developed to the maximum, can be used for many purposes to help others. When the ego no longer controls our lives, we will realize what a precious gift our intuition is, and we will put it to use in every area of our new life.

If you are embarking on a new pathway, do not allow others to make your decisions. Your soul will direct you in every endeavor. If the old fears should surface occasionally at the beginning, it is important to seek others who are on the spiritual pathway. If they are evolved, they will give you love and support but will not try to force you to take a step before you are ready. Your spiritual growth must ***unfold*** like a beautiful flower opening to the sun. Your soul knows the traumas you have been through to get you where you are, and that there is a need for gentle nurturing. It will bring you into the Light at a pace with which you feel comfortable, by putting the right people on your path. They will be ones who have a great affinity with your soul personality, and will lovingly bring you to the culmination point of your Divine Gifts.

For eons the masculine energy dominated the planet, but now the feminine energy is prevailing. The Ascension of Mother Earth is happening through the vibration of feminine energy. Because this energy has been predominant on the planet for many years in preparation for this glorious event, the women have been coming into their power and finally taking their rightful place.

Over thousands of years, many of the souls in female bodies realized that they were stronger emotionally and mentally than many of the men. They hid this knowledge, and played the part of being the **weaker sex.** It was not always wise to allow their superiority to show, as there was often abuse in many forms by the men in their lives. If they were to be considered a **good** wife, they were expected to support the men in their lives in every way.

The evolution of the feminine energy on the planet has caused much dissension among many of the males. They had always been made to believe that they were superior to females, and therefore were in charge of most aspects of their family life and work place. This thought pattern was passed down from generation to generation, and the women were always made to feel inferior to the men. Because the males were expected to be different, they were not allowed to display any traits that were considered to be of the female energy. They may have been very sensitive in some aspects, but showing this side of themselves was considered ***unmanly.***

The tragic outcome of eons of the **superior male** way of thinking was that a man, even from the time he was a small child, was not permitted to cry. He was shamed into thinking that he was not normal, sometimes being compared to a girl. Therefore he tried to hide his emotions from the very beginning of his life. How could we expect men to be balanced when they were never taught that being sensitive and loving, showing their emotions when they were deeply touched, should have been a normal part of the male energy?

Therefore, many males on the planet are having a hard time dealing with this new energy and the fact that women are now considered equal to men. It is also difficult for them to accept that showing emotions is not denying their masculinity – rather it is now recognized as a sign of strength. As the balance is being brought into many relationships, couples are going for therapy to gain a new understanding of the different way their partners think. When I lecture to groups, I often ask the women to be more tolerant, understanding and loving with the men around them. Unknown to most of them on a conscious level, they are working out the trauma of the deprogramming to bring balance and harmony into their **being** and their lives.

Many of the men and women who are awakening spiritually are joyfully accepting their new male/female role. They are learning to nurture each other's needs. More and more men are making the choice to stay in the home and raise their children, while the wife goes to work and supports the family. She in turn, is very happy to be able to balance her male energy in the work place, sensing that her spouse has a more nurturing nature towards the children than she does. They are both getting a chance to finally become whole once again, and are bringing balance and harmony into every facet of their lives. **In the very core of their being, they each have a sense of fulfillment unlike anything they have ever known before.** This is a choice that many are now making. It sometimes calls for sacrifices in other areas, but these are readily accepted when they realize the new feeling of peace they have in their hearts.

We didn't **remember** that we had both male and female energy. The masculine energy has always been situated on the right side of a human body. The left side, which contained the heart and the emotional body, was the feminine energy. Subconsciously, in each incarnation, we were trying to balance both the male and female sides to avoid illnesses caused by this imbalance.

When we experience deep emotional trauma through the loss of a loved one or other devastating events in our lives, we feel the deep sorrow and emotional pain in our left side, at the solar plexus level. This is the area in which the gentle and nurturing feminine energy part of the emotional body, is situated. A releasing is needed in order for us to stay mentally, physically and emotionally healthy. By allowing ourselves to cry, there is a complete releasing of all the pent up emotions in our bodies. When I started my spiritual work eighteen years ago, I would always tell my clients that *the tear ducts were one of the most important parts of our body*, and would explain how important it was to always let the tears flow when we were going through emotional trauma.

We need to **REMEMBER,** that for karmic reasons, we chose the gender in each of our incarnations. Sometimes, after having had several lifetimes as a male or a female, we chose to return in a physical body of the opposite gender. This was often very hard to deal with, as our whole being **unconsciously remembered our lifetimes of functioning through a different energy field.** Often our soul mates, to whom we are connected on a soul level by a deep and abiding love, also decide to return in physical bodies of the same gender we do. As we grow up and are expected to conform to a specific pattern accepted for each gender, it is very difficult when our inner being cries out : **"What you see on the outside is not**

who I really am inside!" They long to be understood and accepted for what they truly are – a female in a male body, or vise versa.

Mankind has never really understood or practiced the Spiritual teachings of two thousand years ago, when Christ explained the concept of karma. He told us that we returned over and over to work out our lessons with those around us. He taught us to not judge what we didn't understand, but we rejected those we considered different in any way from ourselves. He taught us to *love ourselves and everyone else unconditionally,* not just those whose way of thinking and doing resembled our own. He also tried to teach us that **connecting two physical bodies in an act of love was not only our tool for procreation...** *it was also the highest form of glorification of God, in an unconscious search for a deeper part of ourselves.* We were linking as two souls remembering their connection to their Divine side, and for a few precious moments, being in touch with who we truly were as *beings of light*. But once again, Mankind brought this *Blessed and loving* gift from our Divine Father, to the lowest level of degradation we possibly could.

Christ knew and was saddened that we had not understood most of the important teachings He came to bring. He knew that, over time, our judgment of others would bring the downfall of Humanity. Being judgmental is one of our greatest faults, as we are going against the grain of our soul, which is coming from *pure love*.

We are beginning to realize that a judgmental person is someone who has never learned to love themselves. Therefore, the view they have of themselves is projected onto others. The perception is there because of the lack of love in their lives, which could have been a karmic pattern they came to work out in this lifetime. They must understand and accept that on a soul level they chose whatever is happening in their life. They must make the decision to *change their world* through their thoughts, words, and actions. Now that karma is finally terminated on the planet, it is much easier **to turn our life around** – but we must be willing to do so from the bottom of out hearts, and make the necessary efforts.

Thank God, that the teachings by the Ascended Masters coming through at this moment in time are explaining everything, and helping us to have a better understanding of who and what we are. When we have evolved enough to have balanced mind, body and Spirit through applying these teachings in our daily lives, we will see the end of most of our physical and emotional problems. We will be well on our way to once again *becoming Spirit.*

CHAPTER TWELVE

THE COMPLETION OF OUR MISSION

My dear friends and fellow travelers, we *are* living in extraordinary times! Those of us who have started on the Spiritual pathway have felt the quickening of the energy in and around us, and the awakening taking place in every area of our lives.

We have all been blessed in one degree or another in our awakening process. Some are more advanced than others, but the important thing is that we are at least open to all that is happening out there on our planet, and in the Universe.

The events that will occur as we experience the different stages of growth before us will not be easy. Changes will take place in every aspect of our lives. I am who I am – and you are who you are – and no one can take on the lessons that belong to another. Only our soul knows the experiences needed for its growth. But we must give loving support to each other, to at least try to make the burden seem lighter.

Most of us who are already in the awakening process have had many changes take place in our lives, especially over the past few years. We are finishing up the last remnants of karma and, as we do so, many souls around us are moving out of our lives.

This is not done without shedding many tears, because the attachments may have been there over many lifetimes. These tears are needed for the cleansing and clearing of the emotional body, so that we can really advance in the ascension process.

Through the releasing of all the emotions we have held back, which have sometimes taken us to the very depths of despair, ***the gold shall be separated from the dross,*** and our soul will finally take its rightful place as the director of our life.

It is time to detach, my friends! Cut the unhealthy ties to people and things that we feel we ***need*** in order to exist, and that our happiness is dependent on their being there. Please understand that no one shall leave your life experience unless it is time for the changes to take place for your highest good or for theirs – and each shall receive the lesson needed for their soul growth.

There may come a time when we must stand completely alone, as the ones closest to us have not followed the pathway to Spiritual enlightenment that we have, and we feel as if everyone, even God, has deserted us! But ***know*** that we receive the greatest soul growth during the periods we feel are the most devastating in our lives. It is at this moment that we will realize how much we have grown, and the inner strength we have acquired through these trials and tribulations.

Beings from the Angelic Kingdom, and our beloved guides, are very close to us at this time, helping us through these rough periods, because they know how difficult detachment is. We are becoming Beings of Light who are finally spreading our wings and preparing to make the necessary changes in our Earthly lives to follow our destiny path – the one chosen before incarnating.

I want you to know how much you are loved by your beloved guides and Spiritual Masters in the Heaven World. They, along with the angels, have been waiting for this moment to Bless you for having the courage to take this quantum leap into what may seem *the unknown.* Please understand that it was only unknown to your conscious mind, as your soul has always had this knowledge. The Celestial Beings are waiting to welcome and assist you as you enter your new life, taking responsibility for who you truly are as the soul. **Know** that many new pathways will open to you, and you will be led every step of the way.

We must live in the *Now* every waking moment, accepting that the past is finished and there is nothing we can change. We can only release each situation which mentally and emotionally binds us to the past through the ego, by understanding it on a Spiritual level. We must release the guilt, for we dealt with the difficult situations in our lives the only way we could at that moment in time. The lesson was needed for the growth of our soul.

The ego has always been our worst enemy and must be brought under the control of our soul. Our egos almost caused the downfall of Humanity, as it took full control of our personalities at some point in our lives. We forgot that we were **Divine Beings on a Spiritual journey in a human body**. It is time to take back our power by refusing to allow the ego to dominate our lives any longer. We must *remember* that we volunteered to be part of the most unique experiment that has ever been attempted in the history of our Universe. With the termination of **karma** on Planet Earth in 1995, we have Ascended off the Wheel of Karma back onto the Spiral of Evolution. The experiment is over, however, we need to function as Spiritual Beings working for our **highest good** and the **highest good** of all Humanity.

As we help usher in the New Age of Aquarius, which heralds the changes that will finally bring *Heaven down on*

Earth, we must each do our share by ***living*** the Spiritual Laws of the Universe. We must have an abiding love in our hearts for our Father/Mother God in the Heaven World. ***Knowing*** that this Loving Being is always close to us, and we can have a meaningful conversation at any moment of the day or night – is the greatest treasure we could desire. We are His beloved children, and He knows what is in the hearts of each of us. He waits for us to ask for His help. When we do, we begin our journey towards attaining a sense of inner peace like nothing we have ever felt before, but for which we seem to have been searching forever. We must become like little children stretching out their arms to someone whom they sense is a loving person – and God is the most loving of them all. Only ***He*** is our Divine Father, for whom our soul has been searching over and over in each incarnation.

As we become **matter** at the moment of our birth, most memories fade as we learn to function in a physical body. Sometimes we advanced in soul growth in one lifetime, and then regressed in another. At the end of each lifetime, when we returned to the Spirit World, the scales were balanced where karma was concerned. We were faced with what we had accomplished, and where we had failed in regards to what the Divine plan for us had been during that incarnation. We were made aware of the virtues we had planned to work on and had not accomplished. We came face to face with the souls we had interacted with in that lifetime, and often there was great joy or sorrow as we realized if our spiritual goals had been attained, or we had regressed. But we usually wanted a chance to try again. We asked ***The Lords of Karma***, the Spiritual Beings before whom we must appear on our return to give an accounting of our actions in each Earthly lifetime, for one more chance.

The Completion of Our Mission

Before we incarnate, our soul has knowledge of everything we plan to work on, either for our own soul growth, or for the acceleration of another's growth. When we meet our loved ones and the souls with whom we have interacted in our last lifetime, we have a loving discussion as to whether we succeeded in our part of the karmic plan where they were concerned.

The babies that are being born at this time are very special souls. Most of them have their eyes wide open the moment they come out of the birth canal and will look around as if they are searching for someone. This precious gift from God is trying to recognize those around them, to make their soul presence known to them. They look right into your eyes as if they are saying: "Here I am... do you remember the plan?"

As some family members and friends return to spirit at a much younger age than ever before, please understand that there is a reason for this. We choose the time when we will leave the Planet. The choice is made on a soul level and is often part of the karmic plan, realizing the soul growth they can accelerate for the family and loving friends and neighbors who knew them. When a young person passes suddenly, especially in an accident or in some terrible circumstance like those that are happening all over the planet, people are touched to the very core of their being. This tragic event triggers something in the deepest part of ourselves and we are never the same again. Do you remember an event in your lives that changed your way of thinking forever? As you read these words the tears may flow as some buried memory surfaces from your past – maybe as a child when you had buried it so deeply because you knew you could not deal with the emotional pain.

It is time to release all of our old **"garbage"**, my friends. It is time to make peace, at least in our hearts, with all those against whom we have held resentments for some reason or another. Some people have been hanging onto these quarrels or grudges for thirty or forty years. All this **wasted** time, when instead we could have been working on understanding, compassion and forgiveness. We must learn to accept that each individual is different and has a right to their own way of thinking. Ours may be right for us, but it does not necessarily mean that it is right for another. We must at least have respect for the ideas of others, even though we see things in a different light. We must work with **free will,** putting unconditional love in every situation. Imagine how quickly we could bring **Heaven down on Earth,** if each of us on our beautiful Planet accepted everyone unconditionally. If we could feel **loving** energy flowing from each soul on Earth, no one could raise a hand to hurt any living thing. The greed would disappear, and neighbor would help neighbor, remembering the Spiritual truth that *we are our brother's keeper.*

At this unique moment on Earth, we are all experiencing trials and tribulations. Many challenges are being placed before us, and there are only two ways we can deal with them. First, we can allow our egos to trigger the fears and expect the **worst, seeing only the negative side of the situation.** Mankind has been prone to do this since he realized he no longer had the control of his life that he did when karma was still prevalent on the planet. His second choice is to begin questioning his inner self about why things are changing all around him. He must come to the realization that a loving, **positive attitude, will go much further than literally making himself ill through worry.** He will finally learn that there is nothing to gain from this attitude, and will possibly start his search for the answers on a spiritual level.

When you see someone around you that you realize is going through many upheavals, open your heart to them. Sometimes through a few encouraging words, we will touch a place deep in their heart, and ignite the small flame that eternally burns in their soul. Have the title of a book in mind to refer to them, possibly one that started your awakening and your evolution on the Spiritual pathway.

We need to live each day to the fullest, **_knowing_** that we are being watched over by our loving friends and family members in the Spirit World. Even though they may have left the planet long ago, if they have not returned in another physical body, they can come close to us at any time they wish. The love that binds us to another soul is never broken just because they return before we do. When the soul determines that it has fulfilled its divine plan in this incarnation, it will return Home to Spirit. Their departure may trigger much soul growth for those around them, which was also part of the original plan. Consciously, the ones who are left behind to mourn their passing may not see it in this way. They only feel their loss, and believe that they will never feel whole again. Some who lose a loved one late in life never recover from the shock of finding themselves alone, separated from the one they felt was the other half of their being. There is no greater love than that between two souls who have had many incarnations in loving relationships where two hearts beat as one. With the awakening of Humanity, more and more people are admitting that they have had experiences where they have felt the loving presence, or seen loved ones after their passing. They felt themselves being consoled by these spirit beings for long periods after they left the planet. Knowing that they hadn't forsaken them helped them to adapt to life without their physical presence.

As we move closer to the time of the ascension of the planet, we will be able to make contact more easily. The more work we do on our own ascension process, allowing our Light body to control our physical body for longer periods of time, the sooner the space between the two worlds will diminish. Very shortly, there will come a time when your new belief system will seem so natural to you, that you will wonder how you could ever have thought otherwise. You will feel a new sense of well-being, happiness, and joy in every aspect of your lives. This will bring a feeling of inner peace like nothing you have ever known before.

I mentioned earlier in this chapter the importance of learning to live in the *NOW*. For those who are ready, I have requested that a special dispensation from God to release from their subconscious mind all the past life karma still blocking their Spiritual evolution, be given through a meditation. Each of you who desires this must make the request with a sense of **knowing in the very depth of your soul,** that you are exactly where you are destined to be at this moment in time. When made from the heart, the request for this dispensation can trigger the release of all the cords that bind you. We have no time, and there is no need, to spend years in past life therapy trying to work out the traumas from former incarnations. This knowledge is no longer necessary **if our inner being accepts the truth :** *We have always been a Divine soul* **functioning through a physical body, the vehicle needed for its growth.**

****

Start by sitting in a quiet place where you feel close to God, with glorious music, which deeply touches your soul, playing softly. Breathe deeply, to relax your mind and every part of your physical body, bringing you into alignment with your Higher Self. Allow your soul to soar high on a golden beam of light, which transports you higher and higher above the Planet towards the place it calls *Home,* that special site where it abides between each Earthly incarnation. You are at *one-ment* with your beloved Father/Mother God, who has been waiting eons for this request from you. As you sense the loving energy of the Angels, Archangels and Ascended Masters, you will find yourselves surrounded by a violet flame. You hear the melodious voices of beautiful angels singing glory to God. It is at this moment that you sense the presence of that Divine Being, who has known you as the soul since the beginning of time. He holds out His hand, and you put your hand in His. This is the moment that you *truly remember* that you have *always known Him...* your soul belongs in His Kingdom, which is also *your Home.* Ask that you be given the gift of instant memory... that you may *know who you truly are,* so that you may finish the tasks your soul chose before this last incarnation. Bathe in the Light of the Supreme Beings around. Spend the time you wish in your Heavenly Home. When you are ready, come back slowly, bringing with you the memory of this Celestial moment, knowing that you have been truly Blessed.

****

If your first attempt is not as successful as you had hoped, request that clarification be given to you in the dream state. Your ego may still have some control over your life, or blockages in the subconscious mind may be the cause. It means there is more releasing to be done in these areas. God must *know* **that in our heart we are truly ready for this,** because He gave us *free will, and even He cannot take this away from us.* Repeat the meditation with more fervor. When your releasing and clearing is complete, and **your *Higher Self* is in charge of your life –** *you will get your miracle.*

New techniques to release traumatic memories at a cellular level have also been brought forth to help us with physical problems. Once the karmic trauma in the cellular structure has been brought to the surface and acknowledged, the healing of the physical body should begin. The pain is no longer needed if we have understood our lessons. Many Lightworkers are working with these techniques. If physical problems which seem to have no medical reason have persisted over a long period of time, you may desire to consult a therapist in this field.

As we move into the new Spiritual energy that permeates the planet at this point in time, I want you to know how truly blessed you are. We are living in the most important time in the history of Humanity! Our Father/Mother God and his Heavenly workers in the World of Spirit have been waiting eons for this glorious moment – *we are truly bringing Heaven down on Earth, as it was originally meant to be.* Now is the time when all the beloved children on Schoolhouse Earth have finished their lessons, and are finally graduating. We are returning *Home.* Mother Earth is Ascending, and we as inhabitants of this beautiful planet are ascending with her.

Sit quietly, close your eyes, and allow your soul to feel the inner joy that should be surfacing. This feeling of joy should reverberate throughout your whole being. Feel the love that is flowing to you from the Angelic Kingdom, the Heavenly Hosts, and your beloved Spiritual guides – some of whom have been with you since your first incarnation on Earth.

****

To my dear friends and fellow travelers... I hope that by reading this book, you will have realized how closely the world

The Completion of Our Mission ~165

of Spirit – from our Heavenly Father/Mother God to our beloved family members who have returned *Home* to Spirit – are working with us.

The Ascended Masters who asked me to bring you the information in this book, wanted it given in a gentle, loving way. They did not want any fear to enter your consciousness during the awakening process.

I realize that this material may be much to absorb for someone who may have had no prior knowledge of the Spiritual awakening that has been taking place in all the children of Earth. But *know* that, if you are reading this, your soul is ready to take its rightful place as the director of your life, anxious to complete the tasks it chose before you incarnated.

It is a challenging time for all of us, and we must take the necessary steps to move onto our Spiritual Pathway. If doors to the past close, know that new ones will open and you will be exactly where your soul chose to be at this moment in time.

There is an exciting new world opening to us, and we are blessed to be a part of *the most important time in the History of Humanity!*

Give thanks to God for allowing you to be on the planet, sharing in Mother Earth's great moment of joy, as She prepares for Her Ascension. **This means that we will have completed our mission and will also be on *The Pathway Home***

I love you all!

REQUEST FROM MOTHER MARY

My Son, Jesus, came to Earth to suffer, but he is no longer suffering. He was taken down from the Cross long ago, except that the people on Earth continue to crucify Him.

I ask that you stop the Crucifixion that you humans re-live every year on that special day. We want you to remember the Resurrection and the Ascension... that was the message Jesus came to bring two thousand years ago, but was not understood: To let you know that He Ascended back into Heaven when His mission had been completed, and that you will also Ascend when the time is right.

I bring you Love, Peace and the Divine Blessing of the Father/Mother God, Creator of The All That Is, and of Sananda, My Beloved Son whom you knew as Jesus The Christ.

ABOUT THE AUTHOR

Carole Sanborn Langlois has lived all her life in Quebec, Canada. Until her spiritual awakening took place in 1977, she was a successful business woman. At that time, however, she began her spiritual studies in earnest.

Carole's soul rescue work began in 1980, when lost souls began to come through the trance mediums she was training in her classes. Spirit told her she was to help these souls to cross over into the Light. Her first book, ***SOUL RESCUE... Help on The Way Home to Spirit*** describes these personal experiences.

In 1993, she began channeling the Ascended Masters. Most of ***THE PATHWAY HOME*** was written this way.

Carole now resides in both Canada and Fort Lauderdale, Florida. She also travels throughout the world giving lectures and workshops, as well as spiritual healing.

For additional information, please contact Carole at **That's The Spirit Publishing Company's Florida address,** which is located at the front of the book.

How Do We Know That Life Continues After Death?

Canadian author and medium Carole Sanborn Langlois shares many of her personal experiences in this field so intimately that you feel as if you are actually there.

"This book substantiates the fact that more and more souls find themselves in difficulty, having been completely unprepared for death. They awaken in an environment with which they are unable to cope. This is where Carole and her group of helpers come on the scene. This book is compulsive reading material, but be prepared to shed a tear or two. Each case history provides proof that there is an urgent need for groups such as this around the world.

Compassion, hope, love and comfort is experienced on every page, and now is the time for this book to be read worldwide. It makes a positive statement with absolute conviction :
"THERE IS NO DEATH."

(Quote from the Greater World Christian Spiritualist Association of Great Britain)

SOUL RESCUE... Help on the Way Home to Spirit
IS RECOMMENDED FOR ANYONE WHO HAS LOST LOVED ONES, IS FEARFUL OF DEATH OR HAS EVER QUESTIONED THE POSSIBILITY OF COMMUNICATING AFTER DEATH.

U.S.: P.O. Box 2503
Fort Lauderdale, FL 33303-2503
Tel/fax : (954) 522-8317
Internet: whtlite@icanect.net(Carole)
Canada: 3500 Fallowfield Rd, P.O. Box 290145
Nepean, Ont., Canada, K2J 4A9
Tel/fax: (613) 825-0259

ORDER FORM

Please send me ____ copies of Soul Rescue, *Help on the Way Home to Spirit*
____ copies of The Pathway Home, *A Journey into Light*

I have enclosed

in U.S. $12.95 for each book plus $3.50 for P&H for the 1st book and $1.00 for each additional copy.

in Canada $15.95 for each book plus $4.00 for P&H for the 1st book and $1.50 for each additional copy.

NAME : _____
ADDRESS : _____
CITY :_____ STATE/PROVINCE : _____
ZIP/POSTAL CODE :_____ PHONE :(   )____-_____

....

Stamp here

That's The Spirit Publishing Company
P.O. Box 2503
Ft Lauderdale, FL 33303-2503
U.S.A.

[Stamp here]

That's The Spirit Publishing Company
3500 Fallowfield Rd
P.O. Box 290145
Nepean, Ont.
Canada
K2J 4A9

That's The Spirit Publishing Company

U.S.: P.O. Box 2503
Fort Lauderdale, FL 33303-2503
Tel/fax : (954) 522-8317
Internet: whtlite@icanect.net(Carole)

Canada: 3500 Fallowfield Rd, P.O. Box 290145
Nepean, Ont., Canada, K2J 4A9
Tel/fax: (613) 825-0259

ORDER FORM
Please send me ____ copies of Soul Rescue, *Help on the Way Home to Spirit*
____ copies of The Pathway Home, *A Journey into Light*

I have enclosed

in U.S. $12.95 for each book plus $3.50 for P&H for the 1st book and $1.00 for each additional copy.

in Canada $15.95 for each book plus $4.00 for P&H for the 1st book and $1.50 for each additional copy.

NAME : _____
ADDRESS : _____
CITY : _____ STATE/PROVINCE : _____
ZIP/POSTAL CODE : _____ PHONE :( ) ___-___

U.S.: P.O. Box 2503
Fort Lauderdale, FL 33303-2503
Tel/fax : (954) 522-8317
Internet: whtlite@icanect.net(Carole)
Canada: 3500 Fallowfield Rd, P.O. Box 290145
Nepean, Ont., Canada, K2J 4A9
Tel/fax: (613) 825-0259

ORDER FORM

Please send me ____copies of Soul Rescue, *Help on the Way Home to Spirit*
____copies of The Pathway Home, *A Journey into Light*

I have enclosed

in U.S. $12.95 for each book plus $3.50 for P&H for the 1st book and $1.00 for each additional copy.

in Canada $15.95 for each book plus $4.00 for P&H for the 1st book and $1.50 for each additional copy.

NAME : _____
ADDRESS :_____
CITY :_____ STATE/PROVINCE : _____
ZIP/POSTAL CODE :_____ PHONE :(   )___-_____

....

| Stamp here |

That's The Spirit Publishing Company
P.O. Box 2503
Ft Lauderdale, FL 33303-2503
U.S.A.

Stamp here

That's The Spirit Publishing Company
3500 Fallowfield Rd
P.O. Box 290145
Nepean, Ont.
Canada
K2J 4A9

That's The Spirit Publishing Company
U.S.: P.O. Box 2503
Fort Lauderdale, FL 33303-2503
Tel/fax : (954) 522-8317
Internet: whtlite@icanect.net(Carole)
Canada: 3500 Fallowfield Rd, P.O. Box 290145
Nepean, Ont., Canada, K2J 4A9
Tel/fax: (613) 825-0259

ORDER FORM

Please send me ____copies of Soul Rescue, *Help on the Way Home to Spirit*
____copies of The Pathway Home, *A Journey into Light*

I have enclosed

in U.S. $12.95 for each book plus $3.50 for P&H for the 1st book and $1.00 for each additional copy.

in Canada $15.95 for each book plus $4.00 for P&H for the 1st book and $1.50 for each additional copy.

NAME : _____
ADDRESS :_____
CITY :_____ STATE/PROVINCE : _____
ZIP/POSTAL CODE :_____ PHONE :(   )___-____

Falling Inn Love